P|

January 15, 2000
Athens, Greece

Athens, named for the ancient Greek Goddess of Wisdom, is one of the most scattered cities in all of Europe. It encompasses a vast land mass of 412 km2 (159 misq) and is inhabited by more than four million people. It is the fourth most populous capital in the European Union after London, Berlin, and Madrid.

I waited 45 minutes to catch the bus on that gloomy afternoon, and the line 140 just happened to be one of the longest routes in the city. My soccer practice was an hour and a half away, and the city's bus drivers were constantly under various union strikes, so few buses were on the streets that particular evening.

When I finally returned home, I caught my twin brother Nikola and our two friends Kiza and Boki playing a soccer game on a Sony PlayStation console. "Look at you," I remarked. "I pour hard sweat for hours and you guys sit here and play video games all day long. "Cut the bullshit, Vojin," my brother exclaimed, "take the damn controller."
Even before our birth my twin brother and I shared an intense rivalry that permeated our daily lives. We competed against each other at every opportunity and we even supported opposing soccer teams. Video games were no different. So I chose my team, France, and he chose Italy. After a few moments, he got lucky and scored a goal. He began taunting me and, as usual, our friends were getting a kick out of it.

A few minutes later he happened to foul my player in the penalty box, and I was awarded a penalty kick. Just as my player was about to kick the ball our mother burst in looking pale and frightened.

"Branka just called and said they shot your father! Call Paja immediately to find out what's going on!"

We quickly grabbed the phone and called one of our father's personal assistants.
"Hello, Pajo, it's Vojin and Nikola. What's going on?"
"Don't worry boys," he reassured us, "They shot the Kommandant. Everything is fine, don't stress".
I demanded, "where did they shoot him at?"
"HELLO! Pajo, where did they shoot him at?" we anxiously repeated.
Silence again.
"PAJO!" we both shouted. "In the head," he replied in a still voice.

Meanwhile, at the same time 200 kilometers away, a white SUV with flashing blue rotators was heading full speed towards the town of Loznica, near the Bosnian border. A 23 year-old man was severely wounded and needed urgent medical attention. He was a policeman on leave.

The driver of the vehicle was a well-known controversial "businessman." He carried an official State Security Service badge.

"It was just a minor setback," he reassured himself, "Everything is under control."

Everything was under control until they finally arrived at their destination.

Then Vojislav Jekic came along…

To Rade Rakonjac and the rest of our fallen heroes,

Who responded to the sacred call and took the rifle to defend their kin,

Their endless courage and sacrifice shall never be forgotten!

Table of Contents

Prologue

Preface

Table of Contents

Illustrations

1. Breathe Son, Breathe
2. And then Vojislav Jekic came along
3. I Cannot Believe you have never heard of him
4. Son, I know you fooled me
5. They wanna bomb my entire mansion
6. Put your hand down. I will chop it off myself
7. Father VS the Sons
8. I Could have built five of these Villas
9. You people see what my sons do to me
10. I will not go down as a trator
11. He just installed Rade Markovic
12. His officers had no discipline
13. Now you see why I am in this business
14. Love Thy Neighbor
15. Princes of Serbia
16. The most important day of the year
17. God will forgive us, too
18. Maksimir Football Riot
19. Float me 5 bills and I'll run them dry
20. This is NOT a Raznatovic
21. He fetches me 80 grand a month
22. You have no clue how much he meant to us
23. I am not wealthy enough to afford such cheap stuff
24. The one who's songs you listen all day long
25. A message from *Himmler*
26. Body warm up Best with hard work
27. But you are a Partizan fan
28. He must make it
29. The Serbian Dream
30. Beijing Calling
31. But guys... You took the bus here
32. Who is this Grandma here?
33. Casino London
34. We will always help the poor
35. Nobody will steal in my name

36. "Arkan father, Jokso godfather"
37. God - Give me Bayern
38. Rendezvous with Misha
39. I will be the champion of Yugoslavia
40. That's just me revenging Arkan
41. Israel is Our Greatest Friend
42. I don't care if they are Arkan's sons
43. Rade is our Friend
44. We have Always protected our women
45. Founding of the Guard
46. Discipline is Key to everything!
47. I AM the Board
48. Best day of my life
49. I should have never swayed into politics
50. Blood is Not Water

Glossary

About the Author

Coming Soon

Illustrations

Belgrade, Serbia, 1962. Front row, first from the right.

A nineteen year old Zeljko somewhere in Western Europe.

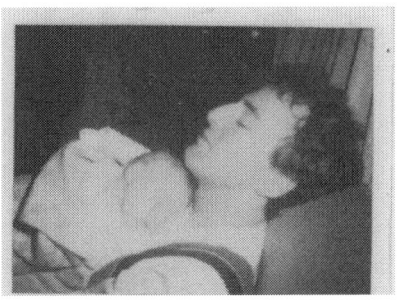

With one of his twin boys, 1983

Grand opening of Grand Casino International, 1996.

As President of the Party of Serbian Unity, 1993

December, 1999. Arkan and the author at the InterContinental Hotel, Belgrade.

Beginning of the Obilic Years, 1997

1988. Saint Steven's Beach was the favorite family destination.

January 15, 2000. Last known picture of Zeljko Raznatovic. Taken approximately one hour before the fatal shots.

Preface

"Why should I be a minority in your state, when you can be a minority in mine?"

Yugoslavia had emerged victorious after World War II when Tito, a communist guerrilla leader, consolidated power and further tightened his grip on the formerly fragile country. Fully grasping the historical animosity and irreconcilable differences amongst the key ethnic groups in the country, he embarked on a national reconciliation program dubbed "Unity and Brotherhood," where all aspects of nationalism were crushed in favor of one nation, one people.

In 1948 he was expelled from the Comintern by Joseph Stalin, and he opted for his own style of communism, dubbed Titoism. He implemented independent foreign and domestic policy, where a neutral Yugoslavia could profit immensely from the Cold war Titans. He founded the Non-Align Movement with Nasser of Egypt and Nehru of India, which grew into a reputable global organization. During this time, a number of substantial economic and political reforms were successfully implemented. A significant degree of free market enterprise was allowed internally as the state instituted a market socialist system. The country finally began to develop a strong industrial sector. Flourishing Yugoslav economy achieved relative self-sufficiency and traded extensively with both the West and the East, while its industrial exports primarily centered on developing third world countries.

The Croatian Spring movement brought a sudden change in the Yugoslav constitution. In 1974, Tito's executive directives wrestled more power from the federal government in favor of the individual republics. This move clearly enraged the Serbian Communists who found their republic split into three entities, with full autonomy granted to the provinces of Kosovo and Vojvodina. Concurrently, the notorious State Security Service began forming special units to gun down the enemies of the regime at home and abroad.

Tito died in early 1980, leaving a rotating presidency to assure the survival of his project. His system, however, began to noticeably crack as nationalist and irredentist voices grew louder with each passing day, opening old scars.

When the break-up of Yugoslavia seemed imminent, the general consensus amongst the key ethnic groups was summed up in one simple phrase:

Why should I be a minority in your state, when you can be a minority in mine?

How This Novel Came About

I never set out to write this book.

I am fully aware that I carry a colossal burden as a direct descendant of Zeljko Raznatovic. I am mindful that the vast majority of people in Serbia and abroad hold a generally negative opinion of him and that the mere sound of his name might instantly evoke the dark decade of the 1990s. He is still considered one of the most controversial and notorious paramilitary leaders of his time whose life is worthy of a high budget Hollywood style James Bond movie.

Under no pretext am I trying to rehabilitate, glorify, or revere my father's deeds, actions, character or persona. This book is not meant to incite hatred or awaken any dark ghosts of the past; nor is it intended to spread nationalism or irredentism of the 1990s that has plunged the whole region into a series of calamitous wars and overall chaos.

This collection of stories is not poised to smear the views or opinions of contemporary historians or anyone else judging the traits of my father. It is not composed to absolve my father for any actions or wrongdoings he might have committed. People are simply eager to discover to this day what he was like as a father, husband, and a man in general. I find it essential to familiarize the general public with the absolute truth and about some of the most ambiguous and enigmatic times of his life.

I would like to take this moment to sincerely apologize to anyone who might become personally offended or shattered by this book. I take tremendous pride in cherishing close friendships with people from all over the world, including some from Croatia and Bosnia. I have always picked my friends based on the content of their character, not nationality, race, or ethnic origin.

Once again, my ultimate intention in this novel was to reveal the flawless truth. This novel was not meant to incite any vendettas or revenge towards the powerful individuals who had murdered my father. It is only justice that I seek, and only through clear and pristine truth can justice be served.

This assortment of stories from his life that I have compiled is simply supposed to be a simple and unpretentious page turner. It is not meant to be a bestseller. If you had expected a comprehensive autobiography about my father, I am sorry to disappoint you, but you are reading the wrong book.

I have purposely chosen to disclose these chapters of my father's life in a short story format, stories which are mostly unknown to general media and common folk. Some of these stories are not wholly about my father, but they relate to him directly or indirectly. I have therefore felt a rightful justification to include them.

Please understand that the entire content of this book is 100% accurate and true to the best of my knowledge, and in case I have made an error or a gaffe, please forgive me for the faulty injustice occurred on my part. It would be a sin to history not to acquaint the public with a man's true colors and the broad spectrum of his dynamic personality. This is the first time you will read exquisite material about his controversial death on January 15, 2000.

Due to the highly sensitive nature of this material, I have received a lot of genuine appeals and major threats not to publish this book. What astounds me is that some people have really underestimated the will, courage and persistence of a son whose father was brutally murdered. I have sat 14 years in shameful silence, hoping and praying every day that the Serbian authorities would finally resolve this murder and bring the individuals responsible to justice. Nevertheless, my struggle is nothing short of just and rightful. I will bear any burden, pay any price, and meet any hardship for the sake of truth, no matter what the consequences.

Ladies and gentlemen, love him or hate him, this is the real Arkan.

Vojin "Jogi" Raznatovic
California 2014

"It's better to die on your feet than to live on your knees."

- Emiliano Zapata

1."Breathe Son, Breathe"

August 31, 1983.

Ten months after my mother had given birth to my sister Milena, she did it again. One can only envisage the euphoria and jubilation a man experiences when he receives the news his wife had just borne him not one child, but a pair of twins! Not only twins, but both males! That has to be the greatest pride and joy for any given father - especially when your proud ancestors are from Montenegro - the "Serbian Sparta" of which my father so lavishly boasted.

As soon as he found out, he gathered a few cars with his closest friends, circled around Belgrade's main square, and fired celebratory gunfire in the air with every weapon he had at his disposal.

When he returned to the hospital he was informed of the gruesome news that his twin boys, born at only 7 months, and with underdeveloped lungs, were given a slim chance of survival.

He Gives. He Takes.

"But not this time!" my father declared. "God gave me two male heads in one shot for a reason! You have got to save my boys!"

The chief doctor arrived to explain that my mother had severe internal bleeding, and they were forced to pull us out at a premature stage of the pregnancy. My brother Nick was only two pounds; I was a bit heavier with three extra ounces.

I can't let God take away the greatest happiness bestowed upon a man.

He quickly ran to the nearest church to pray. He was there all night waiting outside for somebody to open the doors so he could pray under Jesus' icon for his sons' survival. The priest who found him there in a delirious state took him in and insisted he take a small wooden cross back to the hospital and hold it tight while he prayed for the boys' health and well-being. It is no secret that he paced the hospital hallways and waiting rooms repeating, "Dear Father, please don't take back my twins, and I will defend and safeguard your cross for the rest of my life."

For the next few weeks my father spent his days in the incubator room looking down on his two boys fighting for survival. He would first go to one twin, hold the cross and utter, "Breathe Son, Breathe," then rush to the other incubator and repeat the same phrase.

Evidently the Lord heard him and eventually answered his prayers ...

2. "And then Vojislav Jekic came along"

The people responsible for my father's murder were the most powerful people in the country, reaching the highest echelons of the state. Initially, they tried to paint the murder as a typical Belgrade underground gangster shoot-out of the calamitous 1990s, and their carefully organized and well executed plan would have succeeded if not for the unexpected courage of one man who would uncover their treachery. Vojislav Jekic was a chief of police in a smaller town of Loznica. This significant area 120 kilometres from Belgrade served as a smuggling mecca due to its close proximity to the Bosnian border. The regime and many "friends of the regime" ran their highly profitable smuggling operations nearby, hence why Loznica carried such vital significance.

On the 15th of January, the news spread like bushfire that Arkan has been murdered. Vojislav Jekic received a call an hour and a half later that a heavily wounded patient has checked in under a suspicious name and carried no identification documents. One of his informants, Miki Djuridjic, requested to see him immediately. Ten minutes later, Miki Djuricic arrives and introduces the chief of police with Gagi Nikolic and a highly controversial businessman who carried an official SDB (State Security) badge. They explain to Vojislav that one of their men has been wounded, and they would appreciate if he made sure he was given proper treatment and care.

Putting two and two together, Vojislav Jekic immediately rallies his entire police force, and puts the entire hospital under a severe lock down. He placed sentries outside, thus effectively making sure that mop up teams from Belgrade could not arrive in the hospital and finish off the wounded Dobrosav Gavric (who was also a member of the police force).

Vojislav Jekic quickly phones his superiors in Belgrade and informs them that a wounded man is in his custody in Loznica hospital and that he believes he is involved in the triple murder that took place this afternoon in the InterContinental Hotel. Belgrade immediately sent forensic experts to Loznica to verify that the DNA found on the floor of the crime scene matches with the wounded fellow in the hospital. He gets an order to immediately secure the hospital and keep everyone out.

The next day, Vojislav Jekic gets summoned to Belgrade by Dragan Ilic, (the head of the anti-crime unit) in order to receive his statement of the last night's events. Upon handing over his declared account of events, Vojislav Jekic was told to stick around and not leave for Loznica yet. He received a call a few hours later from Dragan Ilic again, who insisted Vojislav Jekic meet him at his house.

After he arrived at Ilic's home, he realized there were a few senior police heads present who openly discussed last night's turn of events. Vojislav Jekic immediately realized that Ilic's tone is different, who now tried to convince Vojislav that last night's assassination was a classic gangster shoot-out. He then orders Vojislav Jekic to go back to the police headquarters and alter his statement that he ever saw a controversial businessman in Loznica with Miki Djuricic and Gagi Nikolic. They told him they are expecting him in the morning at the national police headquarters to alter his story.

Realizing he is forced to lie and cover for his superiors, he refuses to change the version of events in his statement. He is called again and advised that "for his own good it would be better to alter the statement and omit the controversial businessman from his statement altogether".

On his drive back to Loznica, he realized he was being followed by two vehicles. He immediately recognized the state had sent hit men to kill him, so instead of going home, he proceeded towards the bridge on the Bosnian border. Upon seeing an ambush in front of the bridge, he swerved to the left and drove a few miles along the bank of the river. He located one of his contacts, who quickly ferried him across the river to safety.

The head of the national police, Vlajko Stoiljkovic, quickly sacked him and sent out the highest priority warrant for his arrest.

Vojislav Jekic lived the entire year in hiding when he was finally smuggled back to Belgrade in order to testify this important version of events in court. His testimony was the clearest indication how involved the highest state and police officials were in my father's murder.

Due to his highly significant role as a primary witness, his fate was sealed.

After living more than five years in strict hiding, he was finally located and murdered in 2006. His testimony is still recorded and regarded as the key evidence of powerful State figures involvement in my father's murder.

To realize how ruthless this "killing machine" has gone out of its way to cover their tracks is pretty gruesome.

Bosko Buha was a police general who became the assistant head of the newly formed *Department of Public Safety* within the Ministry of the Interior. His immediate task was to begin secretly investigating the involvement of the highest police executives and top state officials in series of controversial murders that took place on the streets of Belgrade. He quickly unraveled my father's complex assassination and decided to act. Somebody tipped off these powerful former officials, whose cronies on the streets managed to assassinate him on June 10th, 2002.

Next time they ruthlessly struck again was on February 6, 2004. Mistaking his brother due to their similar appearance, the assassins managed to kill Dalibor Mateovic. His brother Zvonko was my father's only bodyguard present during my father's assassination, therefore becoming a key witness in the judiciary proceedings.

It is worth to mention that anybody of interest and prestige who had tried to facilitate the investigation and court proceedings regarding my father's murder instantly met the same fate.

My father's two close friends from his youth with direct ties to State Security Service were murdered six months apart in 2001. They collected vital evidence through their former employer and friends in the State Security Service. They dropped of all the evidence to the district attorney was assigned to my father's case, but he was too hesitant to act.

The quest for justice had cost them their lives.

3. "I cannot believe you have never heard of him"

It was August of 2007 when I met Erica in Santa Monica, California. She was an attractive blonde, a petite dance instructor who I had found immensely interesting. Shortly afterwards, she extended an invitation to join her for some margaritas and a dinner at her house the following weekend. I happily obliged.

As I walked into her beach house the following weekend, my eyes immediately caught a glimpse of a framed picture of her dance team with American troops, and the caption read: Tuzla, 1997. After a few hours, she had finally stated that she had travelled to Bosnia to entertain the US troops stationed there. As much as I hoped not to get involved in the standard 1990s political talks, I had realized it was imminent. The mood suddenly took the hit for the worst when she abruptly asked me, "Since you are Serbian, have you heard of this notorious paramilitary leader in Bosnia?" They made a documentary about him called the "Baby-Face Psycho."

"No, actually," I lied. "I can't say that I have."
"Well let's put it on! You gotta see it! It's crazy!"
"Well not now," I reasoned, "Let's watch it next time."
"Why not? I really want you to see it."

You have got to be kidding me.

As we are watching the CNN documentary about my father, she kept repeating, "I cannot believe you have never heard of him! Everybody in Bosnia knows about him and the Tigers. They were the most feared militia there."

Even though I was forced to watch it, I tried my hardest afterward to maintain my composure. I mean certainly another margarita did the trick, but I was still in a state of shock that she made me watch it, short of knowing that that was my father!

Seriously ... What are the odds?

I had arrived home that night, visibly shaken and disturbed. The very next day, Erica kept calling and texting to hang out with her, but each time I excused myself and pretended I had more urgent matters which to attend.

A year later I accidentally ran into her when she curiously wondered, "I really liked you. Why didn't you ever hang out with me after that one night? Did I do something wrong?"

"Erica," I replied, "If you came over to my house for the first time, rest assured that I'd never make you watch a video of your own father."

The poor girl almost collapsed in shock, and I guess out of embarrassment, and simply ran off. I had no other choice but to go back inside the bar and refresh myself with another cold Coca-Cola.

The truth is, I am a Raznatovic and Arkan's direct descendant. I will constantly be reminded of the burden I carry. I am afraid it will always come with a heavy price.

4. "Son, I know you fooled me"

My father had a very difficult upbringing. His father practiced the harshest form of discipline on his only son. My father cherished the moments he could "trick" his father somehow, and other than openly running away from home at an early age, these were the moments when my father experienced a sense of satisfaction.

One trick he played on his father became highly famous. Sometime in the late 1950s, he picked up a local paper and yelled to his father that "Comrade Tito had died." Upon hearing the news, my grandfather Veljko quickly grabbed the paper to read about it. My father just smiled and said "got ya." His father took his head and smashed it on the floor. No father enjoys looking like a fool.

My mother is a humble and honest woman from a small town in Montenegro who, quite honestly, can be less than soothing at times - especially when she would cook a healthy, traditional ethnic specialty which all of us siblings simply detested. This particular cold October day in 1993 seemed to be just one of those days.

My older sister Milena, my twin brother Nikola, and I could smell the distinct odor of sautéed kale from a mile away. As we approached our house, the smell of this green vegetable just kept intensifying, and we could only suspect the worst!

It's coming from our house!

As soon as we entered the house, we saw the dining room table was set up for dinner. After washing our hands and taking our usual seats at the table, my mother entered carrying a large pot of steamed kale and placed it on the center of the table. She smiled knowing that all her children loathe this given dish. She waited ten minutes by the table to see if any of us would touch the kale, and then informed us that our dad would be home in ten minutes, and that we will all be forced to polish our plates.

We shall see about that!

The last time my mother cooked this dish for us, my father ended up "disciplining" me with a belt until I finished my plate. I had to keep swallowing the disgusting vegetable while tears streamed down my face.

Not even a quarter of an hour had passed when we heard my dad's signature Mitsubishi Pajero enter the driveway. He walked into the house very joyful, but then Mom pulled him aside to complain that none of the children had touched their plate of kale.

"You are going to polish your plates!" he yelled. My siblings, visibly petrified, quickly started shoving kale in their mouths. They had to shut their noses in order to swallow every bit of it. Massive tears were flowing down their cheeks, but in this household, discipline was everything. However, observing their torture, I decided that I would not allow myself to succumb to the same type of terror.

Not this time.

The golden opportunity arose when my dad took a whole plate of kale and sat in the living room to watch Inter-Milan, an Italian soccer team. He loved to watch his close friend Dejan Savicevic play soccer and took great pride in admiring his magnificent dribbling skills.

Shortly afterward, my two siblings informed him their plates were polished. He got up from the couch, inspected the empty plates, and dismissed them. "If I were you, Vojin, I would get on with that plate" he hinted. "You know you are not getting up till that kale is gone."

Twenty minutes later I calmly informed my dad that I was finished with my plate as well. He got up from the couch, skeptically took a glance at me while his eyes were locked on the empty plate in front of me.

"I don't believe you ate the whole thing in such a short amount of time. GET UP."

As I stood up, he started searching underneath the dining room table for any traces of kale. When he realized there was nothing, he made me put my hands behind my back, and he began searching my pockets.

Convinced I was trying to trick him, he began patting my waist and even the slippers on my feet. He was very wary of the situation and kept questioning me as to if I had really finished my plate. When he finally realized there were no traces of kale anywhere, I was free to leave.

Later that evening, I heard a knock on my door just as I was about to shut out the lights. Dad walked in and took a seat beside me on the bed. He gazed at me for a few seconds, then finally spoke, "Son, I know you fooled me. I have been thinking the whole afternoon and evening about the kale incident. There is no way you ate that plate of kale, or you would have finished it with your siblings. I know you had an ulterior strategy. I will not do anything to you - I give you my word- just be honest with me. What happened to the kale?"

I inhaled deeply and replied, "I knew you were going to search my pockets, trousers, and even shoes, Dad, so I stuffed all the kale into my hoodie sleeves. As soon as you dismissed me from the dining room, I quickly rushed to the bathroom and flushed it down the toilet."

My father began laughing and gave me a kiss on the head. He told me he used to pull the same tricks on his father, and he admitted he never saw this one coming.

5. "They wanna bomb my entire mansion"

May 1999. The NATO airstrikes against Serbia had entered its third straight month, and my mother, siblings, and I were glued to the TV every day in Greece watching the news. One day, it was announced that NATO might bomb my father's mansion in Belgrade, which was adjacent to his former Serbian Volunteer Guard main headquarters.

The crisis further deepened when my father's best man and godfather, Borislav Pelevic, made a crucial error when he declared to the media that "the Tigers have been deeply engaged in fierce battles in Kosovo." The next day the INTERPOL warrant for my father's arrest was re-activated.

My father had always dismissed the assumption that his Tigers were in Kosovo. He pompously declared that they were still in Belgrade, but grudgingly ready to face any invader that dared to cross the border.

So furious was my father that Pelevic had reactivated his international warrant he heatedly lashed out at him, "You just re-activated my warrant from the Hague! If you weren't my godfather, do you know what would have happened to you?"

My father seemed unaware to the fact that his life was prolonged because of the Kosovo crisis. The newly established head of the State Security made "the removal of Arkan" a priority. (They had briefly suspended their plans until the NATO bombing campaign was effectively finished.)

I tried endless times to reach my father that day, totally oblivious to the fact that he had more serious matters at hand. Finally, as I dialed his "other" number, he answered in a rather thundered tone. "Is everything ok?"

"Well, not quite, Dad. Is it true NATO might bomb your house?"

"I am not sure. I heard it's one of the targets. Why?" he replied.

I said, "Ok, listen to me carefully. This is of utmost importance. Go inside my room as soon as you arrive home. In the left corner adjacent to the door, there is a small hole that you will be able to see. It looks like a mouse hole, but it's not. Please take out the 100 bucks that I had stashed there, and hold it for me. I will come get it when the war is over and I come back for the summer break."

Silence.

All I hear is the media personnel speaking English in the background. Then I hear my father in astonishment and disbelief, "Unbelievable. They wanna bomb my entire mansion and he wants his petty 100 dollars!"

6. "Put your hand down. I will Chop it off myself"

Even though his paramilitary force was one of the most fearsome and disciplined units in the Bosnian War, setbacks and losses were inevitable for both warring sides. Naturally, the Tigers were no exception.

After the Croatian military launched the controversial Operation Storm in August 1995, fierce battles followed in Western Bosnia. A series of well-coordinated and planned offensives between the Bosnian and Croatian armies, supported by the NATO aviation, totally broke the defensive lines of the Bosnian-Serb positions. The ultimate prize was the largest city and the de-facto capital of the Serb-republic Banja Luka. My father and his Tigers were urgently dispatched to slow down the rapid enemy advance and to stiffen the resolve of the demoralized Serb soldiers and irregulars.

Shortly after their arrival, heavy battles raged around Sanski Most in Western Bosnia. The Tigers suffered the largest losses in their history (19 killed and more than 100 wounded), while stubbornly defending the town of Kljuc. As these battles proved to be some of the fiercest of the entire war, morale quickly began to plunge in the Serbian ranks. The Bosnian army's constant artillery barrage, had finally begun to shift the momentum on the battlefield in their favor.

It was during these crucial battles that my father was recalled to urgently appear in Banja Luka in order to discuss the vital strategic and defensive measures put forth by the general staff of the Bosnian-Serb army.

As the meeting was unfolding, he received a desperate call from one of his colonel's that the situation on the front had become extremely alarming, with the army regulars and irregulars guarding their flanks and fleeing the battlefield en masse, leaving the Tigers exposed to the enemy on all sides.

Unacceptable. This is the Serbian Army.

My father quickly rushed back to the front lines; the scene was abysmal. He was stunned by the demoralized and disheartened faces standing before him. He quickly ordered them to formation and immediately attempted to stiffen their resolve.

"I know the situation has become dire. We are getting pummeled every hour of the day by the enemy. The regular army has fled, leaving us and these few irregulars to defend our positions against a superior enemy, but I cannot allow even one soldier to kill the morale and spirit of the others. We are the Serbian Army! We are here to fight! If someone desires to leave and abandon his soldiers in arms, then raise your hand and you are free to go home!"

A dozen or so of the irregulars reluctantly raise their hands.

He repeated again, "If you are scared, raise your hands and leave! You are free to go now."

It just happened that my older brother Michael was present at this crucial moment. He had just reconnected with my father a year ago, and Michael was forced (against his own will) to fight the war in order to raise morale and strengthen the spirit of all Serbian troops in Bosnia. This proved to be too much for a peaceful hockey player from Sweden. As soon as he witnessed others raising their hands to abandon the battlefield, he thought of the good life he had lived before he arrived in Serbia.

As soon as he was ready to throw in the towel, one of the captains from the Tigers, sitting beside him, realized the embarrassment and the catastrophic consequences should others take note of this act. He quickly grabbed his hand, pulled it down, and whispered in his ear, "Put your hand down! I will chop it off myself."

7. Father VS the Sons

My father had always basked immensely in his victories; he simply hated to lose and never quite figured out how to cope in those circumstances. He was the type of person that always had to emerge victorious, whether it was an argument, battle, or a friendly sports game.

If I'd ever had a true desire in life, it was for my father and my male siblings to organize a friendly soccer exhibition. I had been bugging him constantly for two years, but he was always so busy he kept brushing me aside. However, I persisted, and he eventually agreed to a match between a team composed of our friends, my two brothers and myself, and a squad composed of all of his friends. We would face each other on the pitch; a friendly game, if nothing else.

For the longest time, he kept stammering excuses such as, "Son, I would, but I don't want to embarrass my sons and beat you by ten goals." But I knew that my siblings and I would die fighting on that soccer field just to prove that even sometimes a David can defeat a Goliath!

Following a week of mockery and teasing, with the constant ribbing that he was too old to face the challenge, he surprisingly approached me one morning and stated that he was up for the challenge. The battle was set for the following evening.

The famed match took place in a local neighborhood's mini-soccer arena, dubbed The Balloon. My siblings and I casually strolled in not wanting to miss a glimpse of our father warming up with all of his 45 year old friends. As soon as he saw us, he wasted no time in jabbing us.

"Guys, here are my sons. Let's teach them a lesson here today on what experience really means."

Never underestimate one's determination.

And so the battle finally commenced. My brothers and I had all been athletes our whole life; specifically, my twin brother and I had played soccer since we were toddlers. Our friends were decent enough, but fear had settled in, and they hesitated to confront my father and his friends each time they were in a possession of the ball.

"What are you waiting for?" I raged. "Fight on! Let's Go! Don't be scared! Attack them!"

They mustered the courage and the game suddenly took a more serious turn. In only ten minutes we were up five goals. Watching my father rage at his teammates and blame them for every wrong move he made was priceless. He began acting like a team coach, subbing in new players constantly in order to tire us with fresh legs. He did not like to lose, period!

Events took a wild turn when he suddenly picked up the ball with both hands right in the middle of the field, claiming he was fouled.

Penalty kick!

We furiously started protesting the unjust call, but he would not budge! I had no choice but to direct our goalkeeper to allow me to stand between the posts and attempt to block his shot.

I stood on the goal as my father ran to take the shot to score. However, Lady Justice was clearly present, and I blocked his shot. He couldn't stand the humiliation, so he took the ball and shrieked, "All right everyone. This game is finished. Everyone GO HOME. NOW! You kids got fired up as if you are playing against Manchester United! Get out of here. This game is finished."

Rightly so, we ended up teasing him all night for losing the game. Even my stepmother joined the fray and kept teasing him that it was all because he had accumulated a little too much weight, and that he had aged as well. He was visibly frustrated; he could not handle defeat.

The very next day he informed us that he would be assembling a brand new team. He claimed this time his teammates would listen to him and win the game. The rematch was set.

For the rematch we managed to gather the same exact team we fielded in the first game. However, when we glanced at our opponents we couldn't help but notice that my father had mustered an entirely new team, composed of former professional soccer players. When he saw us walking onto the pitch, he exclaimed, "Alright boys, let's play some real soccer this time."

Do you wonder if they annihilated us? Of course they did. Nevertheless, we still managed to put up a fierce fight and even score a goal against them. He was so looking forward to defeating his sons in a rematch, we actually expected him to bring in former professionals in order to win.

I can't express enough how vehemently he hated to lose. Nonetheless, we were content. We managed to prove to him that no matter what the odds, we would always put up a fierce resistance.

It is in our blood, after all.

8."I could have built 5 of these Villas"

In 1996, my father was filled with tremendous pride when his GRAND CASINO INTERNATIONAL finally opened its doors. The casino was never busy, except for the times when my father would send a charter to Israel, which in return fetched a great number of geriatric gamblers for a weekend getaway. My brother Nikola and I had always found it amusing to grab fake chips and pretend to gamble as patrons. Soon enough we had mastered every table game and thought it would be quite comical to go and test our new skills at other casinos in the city. (Mind you, we were only fourteen.)

You gotta love Belgrade.

Our chance had finally arrived when I journeyed to Partizan Stadium to purchase my favorite team's jersey. My brother informed me he was going to wait for me at the casino adjacent to the stadium (also named Partizan). I told him to pace himself with chips and wait for me to arrive.
I hurried back to the casino as soon as I purchased the new memorabilia. I was eager to discover my brother's progress, hoping he didn't lose all his money.
I successfully located him sitting on a roulette table with a massive stack of chips in front of him. The value was equivalent to some $500. I urgently advised him to immediately stop playing and leave. He waited five minutes and then heeded my suggestion.
As we were about to cash out the chips and take a leave, a gentleman in a black suit approached us.
"Are you kids Vojin and Nikola?" "Yes," I replied, "What seems to be the problem?"
"I just spoke with your father. He ordered you both to go home at once. He must speak with you immediately."

We are screwed.

As soon as we entered the house our father greeted us with an infuriated look. However, we could see the hidden smile on his face.

"How much did you boys win?" "Five bills!" my brother cried out.

"You asses!" he boiled. "Who the hell gave you permission to go gamble?"

"Well, nobody," I uttered. "We just wanted to test our skills for fun."

Of course he had to play the fatherly role and teach us a lesson. He demanded we walk outside with him in front of his opulent mansion.

"Do you both see this massive house?" "Yes," we nodded in unison.

"Hear me now - If I never gambled in life, I could have built five of these villas! Understood?" "Yes, sir," we nodded.

"The easiest thing in life is to be stupid. So don't be stupid. I don't want to hear about you going to casinos again. Understood?"

The next time my brother and I paid a visit to a casino was some seven years later in Las Vegas. We sat down at the roulette table and wagered on the same numbers we did in Casino Partizan. In one hour we lost all of our money. We had no choice but to get in the car and drive back to Los Angeles. Nobody uttered a single word in the car.

As we drove past Barstow, I realized how hungry I was as I noticed an In&Out burger joint on the left hand side of the road, and I began scraping some change from the glove compartment.

We didn't even have $2 for a burger.

Suddenly, we remembered our dad's advice and the above mentioned occurrence. We burst out laughing and realized we really felt like asses for failing to stay away from those roulette tables.

Oh well. 'Til next time, Vegas!

9. "You people see what my sons do to me!"

Every June my brother and I could not wait to go to Belgrade and spend the summer with our friends. Customarily at this time our father would go on an unruly rampage, constantly lecturing us on how we don't understand nor appreciate the value of money. We found this rather shocking due to the fact that we had lived modestly in Athens and only received a minimal weekly allowance from our mother to go to the movies with friends. Nevertheless, there was very little one could attempt to do when arguing with my father.
He was always quick to remind us, "In the USA, kids your age cannot wait for the summer holiday to begin! They work for three months and then save their money to last them year round."

"But Dad," I fired back, "This is Serbia, not America."
"Shut it, you ass!" he snapped. "Both of you report tomorrow morning at 0700 hours outside of the main office building at the Obilic Stadium."

"Okay," my brother replied. "And what exactly are we to do there?" "Well, we are always looking for some extra construction labor," he asserted with a heavy smirk.

There goes another unforgettable summer.

The following morning my brother and I arrived to report for duty. My father's soccer team had just won the national championship, so all of his thoughts and energy were fixated towards expanding the team's stadium and building one of the most modern sports complexes in the Balkans.

We stood outside of his office window for about five minutes when a familiar face appeared. It was Vlado Vukotic, the director of the stadium, whose main responsibility was to directly oversee and supervise the construction of the entire stadium. He was ecstatic to announce, "Your father has placed trust in me to be your immediate supervisor. He has instructed me to push you the hardest, sometimes even over your working capacity in order to provide a much needed boost and example to the other laborers. Am I understood?"

"Uh, sure," we nodded cruelly. "You start your shift at 7 am ON THE DOT," he sternly replied. "You are going to be fed lunch at 1:00 pm, and you are to meet me here every afternoon at 5:00 pm to check out with me. Now, follow me to our warehouse where we store all the cinderblocks and bricks for the construction."

Lord, have mercy.

A solid month went by. We labored every day for ten hours and kept our mouths shut. We got along really well with the other laborers and construction workers, who showed a great deal of pity and sympathy toward us when they realized who we were and how hard we worked every day.

The highlight of our day was 9:00 am every morning, when each laborer would provide ten dinars a piece, which in turn would provide each one of us half a loaf of bread with sour cream, cheese, and ham. It even came with a kefir yogurt on the side! Breakfast never felt better.

Our spirits remained high throughout the summer until our friends began mocking us. We barely had any time for them - we were up at six in the morning, returned home at six in the evening, ate some dinner, and went straight to bed. We attempted to make every Sunday afternoon a social day with friends, but they would refer to us as "laborers," and constantly reminded us - "Look at this - Arkan's sons and they have to work like slaves." Even the girls we hung out with started to ignore us because we continuously looked exhausted in their presence.

The final blow landed when all of our friends went to a pool to celebrate a friend's birthday. My brother and I were refused a day off and instead were tasked with carrying cinderblocks all day to the eighth level of an office building that was currently under construction. There is only so much a teenager can take, so finally I broke down and complained to my twin brother, "You know what? This is bullshit! All of our friends spend all day basking in rivers and pools, and we have to mix cement and carry cinderblocks all day? I mean okay, point proved, but we are still teenagers. How long are we going to go on like this?"

"What can we do?" Nikola replied, "You know we'll get our asses beat if we say something."

"Yes, but if we are smart and we let him know in a certain way that this is unfair, what is he really going to do to us?"

"So what do we do?"

"I have a great idea. We have to strike where it hurts the most."

The following morning, we arrived at the stadium and began mixing cement and carrying cinderblocks up to the 8th level again. Our father's office window was merely 10 yards away from the building we were constructing. We would look up and constantly catch him monitoring our progress, so I knew the opportune moment had finally arrived.

Two minutes later, my father, quite baffled, peeked through his office window to witness what was happening.

Unbelievable!

He saw his two sons wearing the Partizan and Red Star jerseys - the very two teams he competed against for the championship title! We were singing the Partizan and Red Star chant songs every time we would find ourselves beneath his office window. So bewildered was he, that he shouted to all his business partners and associates who were inside his office to quickly come to the window and witness the unorthodox spectacle.

Everyone stared at us in disbelief for a few minutes without uttering a word. Suddenly, my father addressed everyone in the office, "This is unbelievable! Do you people see what my sons do to me?"

He smiled afterward, nodded his head, and finally conceded, "These two... I give them props... this was well played out."

Our message of grief and frustration had been delivered successfully.

10. "I will not go down in history as a traitor"

Tensions ran high in Serbia by the end of 1999. Although NATO airstrikes had united all the citizens of Serbia for the time being, the unity clearly began to unravel as soon as the hostilities ceased.

To everyone's astonishment, Slobodan Milosevic had attempted to paint the Serbs as having been emerging victorious from yet another war. His well-oiled propaganda machine never ceased to remind the cash starved citizens that Kosovo had remained an integral part of Serbia. The falsely optimistic cries of "The worst times are over, let's rebuild our nation," (chiefly voiced by the old party apparatchiks) had only turned the masses even more skeptical in these illusionary times.

Holiday spirit was visibly absent from the streets of Belgrade by the end of 1999. During the month of December, our capital was usually covered in snow, and the city truly lived up to the meaning of its name - the White City. However, the mood across the capital was incredibly gloomy.

On one of these snowy winter days, I was returning home with my father from the Obilic Stadium when his *other* phone suddenly rang. (He had another phone because he was told the state kept all his calls under surveillance.) He listened for about twenty seconds to the man with a deep voice on the line, and then suddenly burst out, "Tell him to go fuck himself," and then hung up the phone.

I will never forget the following scene as he caught a glimpse of me staring at him from the front passenger seat. He turned towards me, and then for some peculiar reason, revealed the following, "Djindjic's man is at the stadium looking for me. He claims he's got a letter of guarantees from Schroeder (The German Chancellor) explaining that they will expunge my Interpol warrant... such nonsense."

As I tried to process the shocking revelation, I knew the best response would be for me to look ahead and not utter a single word. He continued in a severely distressed manner, "Schroeder's guarantees…. They think I am an idiot. They just want me to bring them to power."

He looked straight at the road ahead. He stepped on the accelerator and furiously sped home, rushing past at least three red lights.

A few minutes of complete silence had passed when he unexpectedly uttered again, "Betrayal has been the focal theme in the history of our people. They think I am the modern Vuk Brankovic, and that I would go down in history as a traitor? No! Never."

"Help THEM come to power, and then they send me to The Hague…"

He gathered his thoughts for about ten seconds and then concluded, "I will never go down in history as a traitor."

Silence prevailed for the rest of the ride home. Without uttering a word, we took our seats at the dining room table, and feasted on some broiled meat and mashed potatoes.

Approximately three weeks later, my father was murdered.

11. "He just installed Rade Markovic as the Chief of DB"...

It is no secret that my father had deeply entrenched contacts within the highest echelons of the Ministry of the Interior. Realistically speaking, for anybody to reach such high stature a few powerful friends in the government were a necessity. One of his best friends, whom he constantly mentioned, was Radovan Stojicic Badza. Their friendship dates back to the time when they jointly commanded the same units throughout some of the fiercest conflicts in Croatia and Bosnia.

Even though a significant number of my father's friends and confidants have been lost, no death shook him more vigorously than that of Badza in 1997. He openly blamed Mira Markovic, the first lady of Serbia, for his death.) My father was so struck by this tragedy that when his personal safe was opened shortly after his death, a picture of Badza was found inside.

Jovica Stanisic was the chief of the notorious State Security Service. Undoubtedly, he was the most powerful person in the country after Milosevic himself. Badza, on the other hand, was the acting Minister of the Interior, which automatically positioned him as the third most powerful person in the state. (He actively controlled the entire police force.) Shortly after his murder inside a local Italian restaurant, dark clouds quickly began to form over my father's head...

Rade Markovic was the police commissioner for the city of Belgrade at the time. He openly loathed the fact that my father had such high authority, prestige, and stature in the country. He personally undertook a special mission to hinder, and eventually eliminate, my father altogether. But first, the waters had to be tested.

An executive decree had been passed where no individual or groups, except those in employment of official state agencies, military, or the police, would be allowed to carry weapons without the special permit from the Ministry of the Interior. The motive of this decree was blatantly clear; it was designed to target certain individuals, such as my father, who still possessed a number of weapons. (After the dissolution of his paramilitary group, my father retained a decent number of hardened fighters.) The new amendment would obviously heavily undermine his power and position within the country by disarming all his men.

The conflict between Rade Markovic and my dad officially commenced when a police intervention unit arrived in full force and disarmed all of my dad's security units guarding his casino in Hotel Jugoslavija. My father boiled with fury. Occurrences of such caliber had never taken place in the past, and it was obvious to him that some new individuals were out to weaken his influence and prestige.

He soon discovered that the directive was ordered by Rade Markovic (who also happened to be a fiercely loyal servant and a close confidant of the first lady Mira Markovic). He could not achieve much in undermining my father this time, mainly because he was just a police commissioner and could have been overruled at any time by his superiors in the Ministry of the Interior. He clearly understood he needed to ascend to a higher position in the state apparatus in order to effectively pose a threat when challenging my father.

Within a year, however, his ultimate obsession had picked up some major steam. Jovica Stanisic had been officially sacked as the chief of the SDB (State Security Service). After the massive protests in 1996, Mira Markovic, (Milosevic's wife), blamed his inner circle for the fiasco and for critically jeopardizing their hold on power. She believed her husband had become too weak by allowing himself to be surrounded by untrustworthy and incompetent people. She quickly decided to become actively involved in all aspects of policy planning and decision making. Her first step was to replace his inner circle with her fiercely loyal and trusted men. She needed to cement her grip, and it was just a matter of time before the change of guard became imminent.

Mira feared my father's power and influence had become the most serious threat to their rule. She openly detested him and made it well known. (Once, their only son, Marko, arrived at Obilic stadium to talk business, and one of my father's main assistants asked him if "Pops" was happy with them. Marko smiled and resolutely replied, "My father really likes you guys; it's my mother who hates you with passion.")

Mira Markovic finally achieved in hijacking her husband's presidency in 1998. Her first step was to sack Stanisic and replace him with my father's arch nemesis Radomir Markovic. The rest of the "Old Guard" was quickly replaced. She was the new de-facto ruler who exercised complete control and dominance over all aspects of state affairs.

I clearly remember something extraordinary that took place on that breezy December day. My brother and I were sitting inside our ice cream parlor, as our father hurriedly walked in. Upon catching us indulge on some of the best Italian gelato in town, he began shouting insults at us. "You Donkeys!!! It's your Slava today and instead of fasting, you are eating ice cream? Throw that away and go back to the house! QUICKLY!"

The the tone of his voice and his facial expression established that father was in a horrific mood.

It's our Saint Day celebration today... He was never like this before...

When we walked inside the house, my father was quick to grab the home phone and dial one of his most trusted associates Rade Rakonjac (who subsequently happened to be in his home town in Montenegro, celebrating the same Saint). After exchanging the usual Saint Day greetings, father wasted no time in informing him that he needed to come to Belgrade - PRONTO!

The following day, or the day after, the whole family was at the house when Rade Rakonjac walked in. My brother and I were ecstatic – Rade was one of our first bodyguards when we were kids, and we held him in immensely high regard.

The mood worsened, however, when my father took him to the dining room and openly stressed, "I need you to stick around for a while. I need to gather all my trusted men."

Rade, totally puzzled and confused, tried to comprehend what exactly my father was trying to convey. My father looked him in the eye, and in a low, worrisome voice explained it all in a nutshell, "He just installed Rade Markovic as the new Chief of the State Security Service."

Rade Markovic thus became the regime's most loyal and trusted *Himmler*. In a few short years (mostly due to Mira Markovic's intense fear and paranoia) numerous "enemies of the regime" were gunned down or simply vanished under puzzling and mysterious circumstances.

Most cases have never been resolved to this very day.

*Rade Rakonjac was murdered on April 2, 2014, as the final draft of this book was being finalized. He was murdered just as the new government authorities declared they were going to investigate and resolve all politically motivated murders of the Milosevic regime. This book is proudly dedicated to him.

12."Kicked me out of Bosnia because his officers had no discipline"...

The history of the Serbs has primarily been characterized by sheer internal division. The famed phrase "Only Unity Saves the Serbs," has hence served as an ideal that has been deeply embodied into every Serb's conscience.

The most recent schism occurred during the peak of the Bosnian War. Ratko Mladic, the popular general in charge of all Bosnian-Serb armed forces, had openly clashed with Radovan Karadzic, the president of the Serb Republic in Bosnia. The schism had largely occurred due to Ratko Mladic's refusal to bulk into the international pressure and cede more territory to the enemy.(Removing heavy artillery from Sarajevo's surroundings and lifting the siege was another key demand as well.)

The Milosevic regime, which was the sole lifeline of the Bosnian-Serb republic, openly embraced this new peace initiative and took concrete steps to apply the necessary measures. In turn, Radovan Karadzic began openly supporting the negotiated settlement, while Mladic openly rallied against such terms and viewed it as another betrayal and sellout.

In order to force Ratko Mladic into accepting the peace terms, the Milosevic regime effectively sealed off the Drina, the river connecting Serbia and the Republic of Sprska in Bosnia. This precarious gamble, for the most part, had drastically backfired and produced an entirely opposite effect. It further stiffened the resolve of Ratko Mladic and his die-hard followers, who became even more furious and rebellious towards Milosevic and his allies. Mladic went even further, criticizing Karadzic and his officials as "mere puppets of Belgrade."

The lack of unity had begun to visibly expose itself just as the long awaited NATO airstrikes commenced. The main goal of the strikes was to provide air support to the newly revitalized Croatian Army and their allies, the newly equipped

Bosnian armed forces. Without much assistance from Belgrade, the Bosnian-Serb army could not withstand the swiftly fierce and powerful enemy offensives. Towns and villages in Western Bosnia began to fall quickly to the enemy.

Fully grasping the catastrophic consequences of a potential collapse, my father was quickly dispatched to this crucial theatre of war. His main task was to deploy his much feared Tigers and rally our ill-equipped and demoralized forces from ceding any more territory to the enemy.

When the collapse of the Serbian front lines seemed imminent, my father openly slapped one of Mladic's defeatist majors, who had openly showed signs of extreme intoxication in the crucial moments of the key enemy offensives. Nevertheless, no matter how brilliant of a general and strategist Mladic was, his colossal ego could not allow anybody to interfere with his plans or embarrass any of his high-ranking officers. I had overheard my father describe the situation in great detail: "We were dispatched to go and protect the Serbian people who had dwelled there for centuries. After the Operation Storm, the long anticipated series of enemy offensives had finally begun. NATO provided the essential air cover, while the refreshed Croatian Army pushed deeper into Western Bosnia, supported on their flank by the 5th Corps of the regular Bosnian Army. With the situation deteriorating by the hour, the troops of the regular army of the Serb Republic started fleeing the front lines en masse, prompting my Tigers and other few volunteer groups to stay behind. We made a stand in Kljuc and Sanski Most and attempted to halt the enemy's advance… and mind you, I answered an urgent cry and had written consent from the President of the Serb Republic, Radovan Karadzic."

His voice suddenly stiffened as he recollected those crucial days of the battle, "We suffered the biggest losses defending those towns. I had to drive around rallying every available Serbian soldier and forcefully return him to the front lines to fight."

He continued explaining that when he approached a temporary headquarters of the Serb-Republic Army, one of the high-ranking officers emerged severely intoxicated. Upon seeing my father, he began shouting, "Save yourselves, all is Lost! Banja Luka is about to fall! There is no hope!"

My father would have none of it. He slapped the major in the face, ordered him to stand firm in a soldier's stance, and then lectured this fellow.

"We are all Serbian Army!" my dad declared, "and no commanding officer can ever lose his senses and become a demoralized and disheartened leader. Think of our glorious officers during the First World War who faced impossible ordeals. Did they ever give up?"

We all stood in complete awe as he explained how he rallied and transferred these few regiments back to the front lines to defend the largest urban center in Bosnia populated by Serbs.

At the very end of the story, my father surprisingly asserted, "You what happened next? He kicked me out Bosnia because some of his officers did not have the discipline to raise the morale of their troops."

13."Now you see why I am in this Business"

FIFA World Cup is the most followed sporting spectacle in the world. It is therefore fair to conclude that football (soccer) is the most popular sport worldwide.

When my father informed us that he took over a second tier club called Obilic, we all seemed somewhat skeptical.

Just another one of his short–lived fixations.

However, we had greatly underestimated how lucrative the industry of football had become. In barely a year, his club Obilic was promoted to the highest league of Serbian Football.

The feeble, pitiful looking grass field with middle-school bleacher stands had started to transform into one of the most modern stadiums in the region. My father became so ambitious and obsessed with this project, that he would spend most of the day at the stadium, where he was directly involved in all aspects of operations and planning.

When Obilic became a champion in 1998, my father was overjoyed. It was the first time one of the two Belgrade giants, Red Star and Partizan, were left without a title. As shocking as it was to numerous party and state officials, he openly boasted how he enjoyed full control over his club, while the two Belgrade rivals were owned by the state.

Now that the title has been won, my father started selling his top rated players to wealthier and bigger clubs across Europe. He hired Ranko Stojic, a very capable and reputable football agent, to handle these trusted negotiations on behalf of the club. I happened to be with my father one afternoon when he dispatched Zarko Nikolic, a vice-president of the club, to depart for Germany with a ten man entourage and personally retrieve and transport the transfer funds from the recent sale of one of his key players.

The whole day my father was on the phone with Zarko Nikolic, constantly inquiring of the convoy's whereabouts. He seemed exceptionally anxious and nervous, until it was finally confirmed to him that the precious cargo had crossed into Northern Serbia from Hungary. He quickly jumped in the car with his wife and headed out to meet the convoy.

Later on that evening, the whole family happened to be in the living room when my father and his wife entered with two giant duffle bags. When they opened the bags, the whole room froze and became silent.

4 Million deutsche marks!

It was the first and only time I saw this amount of money. I remember my stepmom reaching in and filling her entire purse with cash. After she took the purse upstairs to their bedroom, my father simply smiled at all of us and wryly stated, "Now you see why I am in the football business! One player just fetched me four million."

My father was supposed to sell his star player to an Italian giant for 17 million deutsche marks.

Exactly two days before the transfer took place, my father was executed.

14. Love Thy Neighbor

"Love thy neighbor as thyself," is a deeply embedded ideal in our Christian faith. The following occurrence will willingly affirm this particular notion.

My father took great pride in serving the best Italian ice cream in the city. He had been waiting for three months for a brand new and sophisticated ice cream machine to arrive from Italy, for which he paid an astronomical amount of money.

The mighty sun ruled the skies on this warm summer day, when my father received a call that his new machine was ready for delivery. He immediately left his office and rushed home.

This important piece of equipment was dropped off right outside of our cafe's door, and strict orders were issued for nobody to touch it until he returned home to inspect it.
Our immediate neighbor, Milan, had been residing on our street for more than twenty years. He was a bald, pudgy, heavy-set older gentleman, who loved to leave his house throughout the day and visit a local *Kafana* and indulge on strong traditional spirits. His son Jovan had labored intensely for weeks in order to for our cafe to be constructed by the deadline. As you may have noticed, neighborly ties ran deep on *Sokobanjska* Street.

Upon returning home to inspect the machine, my father took notice of Milan's beige *Fica* speeding down our steep street (an affordable Fiat car, somewhat like a YUGO). Milan pushed the breaks too late and ended up ramming the entire piece of machinery and shattering it to pieces.

Upon realizing what he had done, he stumbled out of the car so intoxicated that he barely managed to stand on his feet. He took notice of my father, whose face was in a state of shock and disbelief. My father looked at him, took a deep breath and informed him that as long as he is okay, the machine damage is insignificant to him.

However, Milan protested. Upon hearing this, he reached down in his pockets and took a mere 200 dinars (equal to some 20 dollars at the time), and tried to hand it over to my father and in a slurred, garbled voice explained, "Don't worry, neighbor, I will take care of everything."

"Milan, it's ok," my father replied, "No need. Please give that money to your wife. You might need it for groceries."

"No neighbor." Milan was persistent. "I said will take care of everything."

My father simply thanked him for offering, and went inside the house. Upon seeing us all in the living room, he explained the story in a somewhat jocular manner, "Poor Milan. Crashed his Fica into my new ice cream machine. He got out of the car, visibly intoxicated and reeking from alcohol, and then tried to compensate the damage with 200 dinars."

We all began laughing hysterically; realizing how comical the story was, my father continued, "I just told him not to worry about it, so I just smiled, turned around and came in."

He took a sip of cold water, and then contemplated, "I guess God didn't want me to keep making ice cream after all."

15. "Princes of Serbia? They don't even speak Serbian"

In the middle of 1992, my brother and I ventured to Erdut, Eastern Slavonia (present day Croatia), to visit our father. The Serbian Volunteer Guard's main headquarters was centered there. My brother and I found it extremely intriguing to venture around the sprawling military complex in military uniforms, carrying air guns and "Rambo" knives.

One afternoon, we overheard our dad's voice in one of the walkie-talkies clearly shouting to the captain who was training us to shoot guns, "Get the Mini-99's back to base in order to change into civilian clothes, NOW! Have them look presentable. I will be there in fifteen." (Mini-99's was a code word for my brother and I. My father's codename was 99)

"What's going on? Who's is coming?" I demanded to know.

"Looks like Franjo Tudjman is coming for coffee," jokingly replied the captain.

"In that case, let me sharpen my knife then!" I yanked back.

Shortly afterwards, the whole Guard was standing in perfect order. A few minutes later, as my brother and I waited across the courtyard by the Tiger's cage, my father's signature black Mitsubishi Pajero SUV barged straight into the complex. It was followed by a convoy of more SUV's and military vehicles. My brother and I witnessed an older lady getting out of the car, followed by two boys our age.

Who are these people?

My father saluted to his troops, and the God of Justice was proudly trumpeted. After dismissing the honorary guard, my father was quick to introduce his newly arrived guests to us. He introduced us in pure British accented English, "These are my twin boys, Nikola and Vojin. They are very honored and excited to meet you, your highness".

He turned towards us and announced in Serbian, "These are the princes of Serbia, sons! They are about your age! This is the first time they came to visit their homeland. Make them feel welcome!"

Princes of Serbia!

It is rather difficult to communicate with somebody who is unable to speak your tongue, especially when coupled with a great deal of shock and confusion. Nevertheless, my brother and I tried enormously to keep those two boys entertained.

I recollect playing catch and hide-and-seek with the princes the following afternoon when my father gathered us around and informed us that we were going for a ride.

Thirty minutes later, we were entering a bullet-riddled ghost town. The destruction was daunting and overwhelming. We all quietly stared as our convoy rode past severely damaged houses and buildings. I managed to catch a glimpse of the name on a placard of this abnormal and frightening city - Vukovar. My father was busy explaining to the princes' mother and her delegation the hard-fought battle that occurred not too long ago. The visitors were speechless.

Upon returning to Erdut, my father escorted the royalty to their suite adjacent to the army barracks. When he finally arrived back to his quarters, I was eager to ask him what my brother and I had wondered for the past two days -"So Dad, are these kids really royalty?"

"Yes they are, son," he asserted. "They are Princes of Serbia".

"Princes of Serbia?"? I cried, "But they don't even speak Serbian!"

This particular interaction occurred exactly twenty years ago. I truly hope for the sake of our culture, history, and tradition, that if we were to meet the princes again, they would converse in a flawless Serbian tongue.

16. "This The Most Important Day of the Year"

Every Serbian family has its own saint protector. In accordance with our culture and tradition, a colossal feast is given by the household on the anniversary of their saint's death. It's called Slava. My family happened to venerate the most prominent and celebrated of saints – St. Nicholas. The date of this commemoration falls every year on December 19th.

Customarily during this time of the year, we would receive the same remark from our Dad, "This is the most important day of the year".

It is difficult to describe his excitement and jubilation on this day. He seemed like a little boy going to a candy store or Disneyland for the first time. He was known to be a prime strategist, and excessive attention to detail was one of his stronger traits. Therefore, laying the groundwork early was quite essential in these circumstances.

Preparation for the feast was quite extensive - gourmet food, top-shelf liquor, live entertainment; my father relished being in charge of every single detail of the planning and preparation.

However, the beauty (or impediment) laid in the fact that all adherents were expected to fast on this day. My brother and I have always looked for an excuse or an accidental "mistake," so we would not fast. The previous year our father had caught us eating ice cream on this sacred day and screamed at us profusely. This year, he constantly reminded us, "I don't wanna catch you two asses not fasting, understood? You can handle a day without eating dairy and meat. There are families who barely have a loaf of bread to get by, so you have no excuse!"

The celebration took place every year at Club Diplomatique, right above our Cafe Ari, which my father had built exclusively for special family gatherings and events.

Originally built to accommodate up to 150 guests at the most, this posh and ritzy jewel persistently surpassed its maximum. Our famed house chef Zika, who was previously employed by Norwegian royalty, had prepared some of the most elegant and opulent dishes to date. (I recollect how startled everyone looked as they passed by the buffet table and took notice of his signature creations.)

There were plenty of various decadent seafood dishes, including lobster, scampi, shrimp langoustine, mussels, scallops, lox, trout, etc. My father never cared to drop his riches for this occasion.

The Black Panthers (one of the most famous live bands in the country) were hired to entertain the guests that evening. My father instructed them to position themselves outside in front of the entrance, so the guests would feel more privileged with the live music playing as they arrived.

At 1800 hours, our entire family would gather in the lobby and greet the guests as they entered the establishment. After snapping a few group photos, I took a peek outside of the door and informed the others to be ready because a lot of cars were pulling in the parking lot.

"If there are people coming," my father yelled, "Why are these gypsies playing this depressing music? This is the house of Raznatovic!!"

He quickly ran outside and began screaming at the musicians, "It's St.Nicholas Day! Do you understand? Don't be embarrassing me with this slow, gypsy music! This is the most important day of the year! Now, follow my lead everyone - *NEMOZE NAM NIKO NISTA...*" *Nobody can touch us, we are stronger than destiny...* (A famous national song.)

So euphoric was my dad that he climbed onto our patio's chain-link fence. He began singing the song from the bottom of his heart while both arms were raised up in the air.

The entire evening everyone sang, danced, and celebrated the ascension of our beloved St.Nicholas to heaven. I must admit it was one of the rare times I have seen my Dad so delighted and unperturbed.

The most important day of the year.

As my father celebrated and sang with friends and family, dark forces were watching his every move from the distance and planning the next attempt on his life. Very few people knew it was the last time he would be giving thanks to his beloved Saint.

17."Well in that case, Father, God will forgive us, too!"

My dad was a devout Christian. "Our Father" was recited from his lips every time he sat down to eat, as well as each night before he would fall asleep. He would always proudly proclaim that he was fighting for the Cross and the Serbian People. He would openly state that the only two people he feared were his wife and the Patriarch of the Serbian Orthodox Church.

One of the founding pillars of our Orthodox faith is the subject of lent. Every devout believer ultimately becomes a vegan for the duration of the forty day period preceding Easter. My father proudly fasted every year. He also boasted it was the only time he managed to drop weight and feel more comfortable. He attempted numerous times to force everyone else in the family to follow his example, but the efforts proved futile each time.

I had mustered all my bravery to question how he managed to fast in jails during his youth. His reply was that he only broke lent once in the past 25 years. He never tired from repeating his famous narrative when he liberated a mostly ethnic Serbian town in Bosnia. He would force his entire army to fast, so his soldiers were constantly craving meat and other vital nutrients the body needed to sustain their rigorous training and combat readiness.

A day after a certain town was liberated, a local priest was informed that the Tigers wished to arrive at the church and pray for the wounded and the recently deceased men killed in action. I heard my father recount the story on different occasions:

"So I arrived with my Tigers to the church. I walked in, and there was no one inside. I was told by one of the townspeople that the priests are eating lunch in their dining center right around the church." He slowly chuckled as he continued, "So as I am walking around the church, my nose could not disregard the heavy aroma of a roasted lamb. I thought I was delirious. As I burst inside their lunc room, the priests stared at me in disbelief, as if the Devil himself had appeared. Their beards and fingers were sticky from the rapid consumption of the meat."

"So did you just walk away?" someone wondered curiously. "Definitely not!" he asserted, "I asked them if this was some kind of a joke. It's the middle of lent and they are feasting on a roasted lamb!"

He explained how suddenly the head bishop stood up, took his palm, and declared loudly, "God will forgive us." To which my father responded, "Well in that case, father, God will forgive us too!"

He ordered all of his soldiers to enter the lunch room. The feast had begun.

God will forgive us too!

The lent was officially broken, but at least the soldiers were well fed.

18. "The Maksimir Football Riot"

Of the numerous questions people ask about my father, one of the most frequent lies with the controversial Dinamo Zagreb - Red Star Belgrade football match that was to take place on May 13, 1990. I was a six year old child when we tuned in to watch the live coverage of the football game and watched as some of the worst riots in the history of football occurred.

My brother and I were lucky to hear the whole story from Zonja who was one of the deputy leaders of the Delije, the most fanatical supporter group of Red Star's.

As he was teaching my brother and I how to play a basic game of poker, we began bombarding him with questions about the world of Hooliganism and the trips abroad he had to undertake to support his team.

After hearing numerous stories about their infamous trips to Glasgow, Dresden, Munich, and Zurich, I had to ask where he felt they received the most hostile reception.

"There is no doubt that the most hostile reception has always been on our trips to Zagreb and Split" he confidently exclaimed, "It wasn't even a foreign country, but the same one we all grew up in." "Were you in Zagreb when the riots took place?" I inquired. "Of course I was" he fired back. "Can you tell us the whole story, please," my brother begged. "Dad didn't share the details with us."

"Well, as you may know, the match was scheduled to take place a few weeks after Tudjman's HDZ party came to power in Croatia," he started explaining. "The tensions ran so high, because we all knew that it wasn't just a football game between Dinamo and Red Star, it was a prequel to a continuation of a deeply vicious struggle between Serbia and Croatia." Our eyes, wide open in amazement, simply stared at him without uttering a word.

"Around 4,000 of us had arrived in Zagreb by train in the early morning hours," Zonja continued. "We were ready for trouble because we knew that tensions were high and we were hardcore Serb Nationalists and they were hardcore

Croatian Nationalists. We knew that something big was brewing, so we came well prepared." "You mean you brought weapons just in case," I interrupted.

"Not just weapons. Of course we brought knives, Molotov cocktails, and guns just in case. But we also brought more than 200 license plates from Belgrade. A few hours before the game, our men ventured around the Maksimir stadium, and switched all the license plates on the local cars with the ones we brought from home. The Dinamo fans ended up smashing 200 of their own fans' cars thinking they were ours!"

"Keep going please!" we demanded, "tell us more."

"So all day we had little skirmishes around Zagreb with their fans, but the real trouble started when we arrived at the stadium. Mind you, there was no more Yugoslavia. We chanted Serbia, and they chanted Croatia. We called them Ustashas, and they called us Chetniks. The actual fighting started when a small group of the Croatian fans started pelting us with rocks, so we broke down the barrier fence, and rushed at them. We ended up throwing many of them over the stands straight onto the street, while we chased the rest all the way to the side where the majority of their fanatical fans were situated. We tore out all the chairs and started throwing them at them. They were heavy, so when you threw one at somebody, it was as powerful as a cinderblock hitting your head."

"So where was our dad this whole time?" we asked.

"Your dad was not in the stands with us. He was our leader but he had a more prominent role. He was hired by the State Security to protect the players of Red Star. Your father played a crucial role here. When Dinamo fans broke the fence and overwhelmed the feeble police force at the pitch, your father stepped in and rallied the entire police force on site in order to protect the players and our fans. When the stadium was finally emptied and we were on our way back to Belgrade, we all realized one thing. The war had officially begun."

A year later, the first shots were fired in Krajina and Slavonia. The battlefield had officially shifted form football stadiums to villages and cities. These same fans were officially on the opposing sides once again, but instead of pelting rocks and chairs wearing football jerseys, they donned full military fatigues and fired bullets and grenades at one other.

19."Float me 5 bills and I'll run them dry"

My father had a tireless gambling addiction in the 1980s. Tito, the long-time ruler of Yugoslavia had just passed away, and a lot of underground casinos and gambling joints had begun to appear throughout the country.

Long live democracy!

The most notorious "games" took place in Zagreb, Croatia, and my father would frequently pay this city a visit. It was only a few hours by car from Belgrade, where he resided. It was known that so monstrous was his gambling addiction, he would leave Zagreb at certain intervals and drive all the way to Belgrade just to give his twin boys a bath. As soon as the kids were asleep, he would be back on the freeway. A few hours later, he would casually reappear in Zagreb, as if nothing had happened.

When casinos officially sprung up in Zagreb, my father quickly became one of their most frequent guests. Roulette was by far his favorite game, and his obsession with number 17 was legendary. He has always boasted that number 17 made him either rich or poor.

He was in a local Zagreb casino when he unexpectedly lost a hundred thousand Deutsche Marks (85,000 dollars.) He became even more furious when the casino manager refused to grant him a line of credit so he can re-try his luck. He paced intensely around the casino looking for a familiar face to lend him some quick cash. A few moments later, he spotted one of his close friends (a well-known singer at the time.). My father wasted no time, "Hey, Knight, how much cash you got on you?" "Not more than five hundred deutsche marks from the last night's concert, "he replied. "Float me five bills. I will run them dry."

The rest of the night has become quite mythical. We all know how luck works in mysterious ways. He placed 200 marks on number 17, and the ball suddenly landed right there. He placed the seven thousand marks of his winnings again on the same number, and against all odds, it hit again! He had just won $245,000.

However, this wasn't the end. The young dealer (possibly from shock and total disbelief), accidentally paid him double the winnings. After realizing the mistake, my father and his friends quickly raced to the cage to cash out their winnings.

Upon leaving the casino in euphoria, my dad turned over to Knight and with a huge grin on his face quickly reminded him of the strange intuition he ha experienced earlier.

I told you I was gonna run them dry.

20."This is NOT a Raznatovic"

Long before my oldest brother Michael got married and had a beautiful daughter, he was in a relationship with a notable Belgrade socialite. Not too far into their romance, she suddenly informed him that she was pregnant. Michael, (young and careless he was), quickly located our father to convey the joyful news. However, our father (despite the jubilation of becoming a grandfather), showed extreme signs of doubt and caution. He had heard numerous stories about the so-called "mother-to-be." Nevertheless, he would have never disrespected his children and openly question his son about his girlfriend's loyalty and ethics.

Nine months had finally passed, during which Michael showed a great deal of tenderness and care toward his girlfriend. He could not hide his delight when he became a father.

It's a Boy!!

My father, as the patriarch of the family, was immediately informed that his grandson had been born. He rushed to the hospital to meet the newest member of our clan.

Upon arrival, he found Michael waiting for him in the hallway, holding the newly born baby. As Michael proudly handed him the grandson, my father displayed a great deal of hesitancy and skepticism as he was closely examining the boy. The very first sign was the dark color of the baby's hair. While both parents were naturally blonde, the baby had incontestable pitch black hair.

My father decided to lift him up and examine closely the baby's body shape, eyes, hair, nose, and head. Fifteen seconds later, he handed the baby back to Michael and resolutely declared, "Son, this is NOT a Raznatovic. This baby has nothing to do with us. Please go get a DNA test immediately and see for yourself."

Offended and confused, Michael found himself in a state of shock and disbelief. He could not possibly have imagined that there was the slightest chance this baby was not his child. He became so adamant to prove my father wrong, that he decided to have a DNA test conducted at the earliest opportune moment.

Eventually, the day arrived when Michael rushed to my father's house to speak with him. He greeted my father, shamefully admitting, "You were right, Dad. He is NOT a Raznatovic"

21."He fetches me 80 grand a month"

A few weeks before my father was murdered, my brother Michael was lounging in the upscale Hotel Hyatt with our stepmother, her sister, and Mario, one of my father's close "friends" and business partners. The atmosphere was quite relaxing and peaceful. They were eating some quality cakes and sweets while waiting on my father to conclude an important meeting.

Mario was one of the greatest sycophants and bootlickers I have ever met in my entire life. He constantly followed my father around, and every time my father would crack a joke, no matter how funny it was, he would be laughing hysterically. When my father would cuss somebody out, Mario had to cuss him out afterwards.

This same man lavishly showered me with cash every time he saw me (of course, only so my father would take note of it). His status and position in my dad's inner circle was well sealed. (Surprisingly enough, as soon as my father was murdered, Mario was never heard from again.)

Cutting back to the story, my brother Michael owned a cellular device repair and sales store in one of the most popular shopping plazas in Belgrade, the Cumicevo Sokace. Right across from his store was a money exchange outlet, owed by two brothers from Montenegro. One of them was happily married to an attractive Belgrade socialite, Xenia. My brother Michael and she were close friends and they would usually chat outside of their stores when business was slow.

Suddenly, as they were eating cakes, Mario edged closer to Michael sitting on the sofa. He abruptly made an impolite inquiry, with a heavy smirk on his face, "Hey Mike, between us, how many times did you tap Xenia?" "Are you serious right now?" Michael responded, "That's not even funny. Don't ask me crap like that!"

"Okay, don't be mad... I won't ask you again, ok," he replied.

Ten minutes later, Mario picked at him again, "Hey Mikey, just tell me how many times you tapped it?" "What's the matter with you!" cried Michael. "Have some respect! She's a married woman and I am close friends with her husband! That's how rumors start, so again, don't ask me about bullshit like that!"

"Okay Mikey," Mario teased, "Don't be mad because I asked. "Do me a favor, and just leave me the fuck alone".

Some people simply do not know when to stop. After bugging him for the third time, Michael finally stood up and thundered at Mario in front of everyone, "I have asked you repeatedly to stop bugging me about bullshit and you keep disrespecting me! Who do you think you are? SHUT UP and don't say another word to me, you understand?"

Mario, visibly embarrassed in front of others, suddenly excused himself and left. It took a solid minute of silence for the awkwardness to disappear.

When my father arrived, they immediately briefed him on Michael's "uncontainable outburst" at Mario, and the general embarrassment they suffered because the whole lounge turned their eyes towards their table. Without allowing Michael to explain himself, my father instantly slapped him in the face. Michael was so shocked that he just got thumped in the face over a man like Mario and what hurt him the most was my father's impulsive reaction, not allowing his son to clarify the situation accordingly. My father angrily asserted, "You donkey, he fetches me eighty grand a month, and you think you can treat him like that? Get out of my sight; I don't want to see you. Get lost!"

Regrettably, this was the last contact between my father and his oldest son. They never spoke again.

A few months later, Michael kissed my father's coffin and paid his last respects.

22. "You have no clue how much he meant to us"

My father's funeral seemed to be a well-planned and coordinated media event. I suppose no person of such caliber had been assassinated in the past decade. Borislav Pelevic, who my father officially terminated all contacts with during the NATO bombing of Serbia, took upon the ceremonial role as the family spokesman and the chief coordinator for his burial.

During the entire week of the funeral, whether for the commemoration service or the actual burial, Pelevic proudly wore his Serbian Volunteer Guard uniform. (He even declared himself a "General" of the guard). In the meantime, he callously wasted no time in crowning himself as my father's unchosen successor.

On the morning of the funeral, we were all gathered by our stepmother, who insisted no member of the Raznatovic family "drop one tear." We knew that due to the extensive media coverage of the event, all eyes would be focused on us, primarily on the new widow.

That gloomy morning, we despondently departed for the Central Cemetery, soberly prepared to say goodbye to our father for the last time. Our convoy consisted of more than twenty cars, and it was no surprise that it took us about thirty or so minutes to reach the destination.

Upon arrival, I couldn't help but notice the plethora of people waiting outside. We quickly rushed to the main chapel, with thousands of people pushing and prodding one another in order to get a better glimpse of my stepmother and the children. Even though the plan was to stand around the casket for a mere hour and accept condolences from the well-wishers, it was quite clear to all of us that sixty minutes would simply not suffice to greet all the passionate and hard-stricken people dropping in to pay their final respects.

There was barely a whisper in the chapel as people circled around to express their sincere condolences. The noiseless ambiance drastically altered when buses had arrived from the "other bank of Drina" (as we Serbians called the Serb entity in Bosnia).

The following sight had become quite surreal when tens of wailing women and men rushed into the chapel to pay their respects. It was quite bizarre to witness these Serbians from Bosnia moaning and howling in anger and frustration. We all stood dazzled, perplexed with the sudden turn of events.

"Your father liberated my town of Zvornik!" wailed a stocky woman.

"Your father saved my whole family in Western Bosnia in 1995," cried a mother with two kids.

"Your father fed my hungry kids during the winter of 1993!" shouted a middle-aged man.

An hour had passed when suddenly an older woman appeared, followed closely with what seemed to be five of her grandchildren. She sharply stared at the corner where my brothers and I were standing. She approached us and exclaimed with full tears, "You have no clue how much he meant to us. I am from Bijeljina, and these are my grandchildren. My three sons were all murdered by the Muslim extremists. We were all doomed, until your father arrived with his Tigers and liberated the whole city. He saved numerous lives and families."

She took a moment to wipe her tears and compose her thoughts. She broke down again, concluding, "To all of us across the Drina, you simply have no clue how much he really meant to us."

When the elderly lady walked away, my brothers and I stared at each other in disbelief.

Suddenly, there was a great sense of pride and wonderment in our hearts.

I was beset by truth and justice, rather than vengeance when I kissed my father's grave that day. I solemnly swore I was going to expose all the facts about his life, as well as the complete background of his assassination.

The day of reckoning has finally arrived 14 years later.

23. "I am not wealthy enough to afford such cheap stuff"

On January 15th, 2000, my father was headed to the Intercontinental Hotel, a ten minute drive just across the main river from his house. His wife had recently launched a new album, so my father really enjoyed one of her signature new songs "Dokaz" (Proof). He showed no shame singing it loudly from the top of his lungs. Surprisingly, he was alone again in his legendary bulletproof Chevrolet Suburban. He was oblivious to the fact that in the past few months, he had narrowly escaped three assassination attempts. The state operatives followed and scanned his every move.

For a few weeks, it was obvious that he had let his guard down. I heard him a few times mentioning how he was invincible and untouchable, declaring proudly, "I am Arkan!" He evidently lost his natural instinct and that vital sense of caution that had served him right numerous times in his life. He clearly had forgotten the number one rule in the book of survival - hyenas only attack when they sense a lion's guard is down.

His security detail was composed of the fiercest and most loyal fighters under his command. When my brother and I arrived from Greece that solemn winter, we barely knew anyone in his bodyguard unit. The most shocking surprise was - they weren't even armed anymore and there were only a few!

His mood was jovial as he arrived to the InterContinental hotel. He knew that a Chinese state delegation was staying in the hotel, so he calculated there was no need for any extra bodyguards. The State security would fill the hotel with their personnel to safeguard the foreign entourage.

He parked his car in his usual reserved spot and strolled inside to meet his friends. Manda and Dragan waited for him at one of the booths. They were also surprised to notice that my father had recently begun arriving without his full security detail. Nonetheless, they received the same reply from him – "I am Arkan!"

Because the official state delegation from China was stationed in the same hotel, my father wasn't surprised to see so many strange faces walking around. He figured they were state operatives protecting the foreign statesmen. What caught his attention that particular afternoon was a scrawny looking man in his 20s sitting directly behind him in one of the foyers.

"Who's that behind me?" he demanded to know.
"Nothing to worry about," Manda reassured him. "He is our guy. He is with Jorga and Gagi."

As the trio was sipping on their juices, Jorga approached the table and insisted my father step outside of the hotel to catch a glimpse of his loaded AUDI A8 sedan. He claimed he wanted to sell it to the right buyer. Just as they stepped outside, Jorga seemed nervous as he tried to boast the car's advanced features. Zvonko, my father's only bodyguard that day, closely watched the unknown men standing outside of the entrance.

My father was not impressed. He clearly showed no interest in this loaded machine, so he cut him short, smiled, and politely replied, "I am not wealthy enough to afford such cheap stuff."

Unaware that this was The Plan to gun him down, my father simply walked back inside the hotel and rejoined his friends at the booth. He was joined by Ljuba Shiptar, the head of the Komercijalna Bank who secured him continuous loans for his stadium construction. The assassin teams quickly realized they needed to alter their mission, and they phoned for further instructions.

Shortly afterward, Ceca arrived with her sister. Zvonko stood directly behind the booth, his eyes fixated on the couple of men drinking juices. Just as Ceca and her sister took a leave to go shopping at their favorite boutique La France, my father ordered Zvonko to follow them and provide assistance with their shopping bags. The last few minutes of his life were finalized as the window of opportunity for the operation suddenly appeared wide open.

What my father failed to realize was that he was being closely watched by a few groups of men. Suddenly a too familiar face approached the booth and greeted my father. Just as he walked away, witnesses claim an assassin walked up directly behind my father and fired three bullets into his head. At the same time, they aimed at the two friends sitting with my father. Upon hearing the shots, my father's bodyguard Zvonko quickly rushed out of the boutique and began firing at the assassins near the booth. He shot one of the killers and managed to dodge a few bullets before finishing his clip. He quickly rushed back to the boutique and grabbed a gun from my stepmother, who always carried a Beretta in her purse. He rushed back and shot another man as he noticed the previous target crawling toward the exit door, leaving a bloody trail behind him.

When the gun shots subsided, my stepmom and her sister rushed to the booth in order to get my father immediately to the hospital. As he was fatally spitting blood and diminishing signs of life, Ceca was hysterically yelling for help. To her astonishment, everyone merely stared at her, declining to help. A police unit that "miraculously" appeared on the scene refused to transport my helpless father to the emergency room. It was pure luck that a random bystander approached and offered to drive my father to the hospital.

The organizers of the assassination had hoped to paint the murder as another typical gangster shoot-out. Their mop-up teams were already on the scene destroying vital evidence to cover the official state involvement. They were sent by two powerful police heads, Dragan Ilic, chief of the UKP anti-crime unit and Vlajko Stoiljkovic, who was the head of the entire police force.

Zvonko Mateovic, my father's bodyguard, was spotted pacing back and forth in the hallway of the hospital as doctors tried to do the impossible and save my father's life. He kept murmuring, "I swear I killed one and I wounded one."

There was indeed a fourth person killed inside the hotel. It remains a top secret hidden from the public. His last name was Gardasevic. It has never been mentioned in the media, even though a few witnesses claim they spotted a lifeless body roughly 15 meters from the bloody booth.

His name and role on that particular day were never mentioned. He was employed by the Ministry of Internal Affairs and had been chosen to provide assistance on that particular afternoon in the riskiest of operations, along with many other policemen and state operatives.

His family was informed he died servicing his country in one of the clandestine operations in Kosovo.

The state hoped their involvement was never going to be suspected or discovered.

Then the call came from Loznica that threw them completely off guard.

"The One whose songs you listen to all day long"

June 1994.

Our parents, always strict, kept pushing my brother and I to regularly practice soccer, swimming, and karate; we even attended the most prestigious drama school in Belgrade. Not even during the long summer break were we allowed to enjoy the warm weather and bask in the city's public pools.

Why can't we once have an unforgettable summer?

My brother and I had just arrived home from swimming practice when we realized something was wrong. We walked into our house and spotted ten packed bags in the living room. Suddenly, our mother stormed in from the upstairs floor and hurriedly demanded we pack all of our immediate belongings in our backpacks.

"Hey guys, I am taking the walkman, who has Ceca's tape"? I wondered. "I do," answered my sister, "I'll bring it."

Out of all the up and coming folk singers, Ceca was by far our favorite. That year she was reaching the height of her popularity, with only Dragana Mirkovic and Mira Skoric more popular than she. My brother and I chatted with her the previous October when the Serbian Volunteer Guard celebrated its two year anniversary. She was headlining the event, and apparently the same night, ended up in my father's room.

We hastily packed and found ourselves in a Mitsubishi Pajero speeding towards downtown. A few minutes later, we arrived in front of the main train terminal. My siblings and I thought we were traveling to Montenegro, where most of our extended family from both our mother and father's sides resided. Nevertheless, something felt very odd. Our Mom had rushed us out of the house and appeared very sorrowful. I could never have imagined that she was in a race against time to avoid my father who had just informed her he was on his way home from the front lines.

When we boarded our train compartment, I was too busy browsing my FIFA World Cup sticker book when my mother informed us we were headed to Vienna, and then on to Rome. All three of us were in a state of bewilderment. Still more confusing - we noticed our last name was changed when Mother handed us our passports. It was now Martinovic instead of Raznatovic. Even though we were only ten, our instincts told us that something was very peculiar about this whole journey.

A few weeks had passed, and despite our mother pretending everything was normal while visiting Vienna, Rome, and Paris, we finally managed to decipher the root of the awkwardness and the ultimate reason for our hasty European excursion. We were vacationing in the small spa town of Fiuggi, Italy, when we caught our mom shouting and screaming on the phone in the middle of the night. We recognized our Dad's voice on the other line, trying to console her, "Please Natalija. Don't do this; we have four kids together. I swear I will kick her out! Please come back!"

When she finally realized that all of us were awake and listening, she hung up the phone and walked right over to us. She finally explained, "I have heard numerous stories that your father was having an affair. I chose to ignore it because I know how much people love to gossip and speculate. But Alex called and admitted that the reason your father didn't come with us to Kopaonik this Christmas was because he spent time with her instead."

"Who is the woman, Mom?" we all eagerly requested.
The reply was quick, "The one whose songs you listen to all day long."

25 . A Message from *Himmler*

"The Biggest enemy of the Serbs are the Serbs themselves" - Serbian proverb

The Romans argued that an opportunity arises in every tragedy. Borislav Pelevic, the self-proclaimed "General" and President of the Serbian Unity Party, fully subscribed to this notion. He quickly aimed to exploit our family's horrific misfortune in order to advance his personal agenda while at the same time solidifying his standing and popularity on the political scene. He was, after all, the first person who stated publicly that my father was murdered by the CIA and the powerful Albanian lobby in Washington.

The fact of the matter is, we all knew as early as the next day the identity of my father's murderers. The initial planning, organization, and cover up of this entire highly classified and well-coordinated operation was headed by the SDB (State Security Service*)*. They used Zoran Uskokovic Skole's group of thugs to play off the murder as yet another casualty of the gangster feuds so prevalent in the 1990s and therefore effectively exterminate any suspicions leading to their department. (Skole was too blind to realize he was used as the sacrificial lamb in this villainous endeavor.) The greatest moral transgression of the time had to be the full page obituary he took out in the daily newspaper which read, "To my brother Arkan, may your glory be eternal." This was a towering humiliation for the whole Raznatovic family.

Nevertheless, Borislav Pelevic continued to maintain his more than necessary contacts with the high-ranking government and State Security officials. He either refused to believe that the State Security Service was directly involved in my father's murder by utilizing their street cronies and thugs, or he simply understood he had little choice but to cooperate and accept their version of the story. The fact remains they needed a man close to Arkan who could corroborate their side of the story and avert any assumptions of the regime's direct role in the assassination. Borislav Pelevic began to be regularly summoned by Buca Djuric (the head of the UPK – administration of anti-crime police - who became a de-facto Goebbels of the regime in the cover-up). Therefore, Pelevic was used as a propaganda tool of the regime in order to sway suspicions that the State had any sort of involvement. He was ordered to publically declare that it wasn't a Serbian hand that had ordered my father's removal, but a foreign intelligence service and the Albanian lobby from Washington.

I will never forget when he excitedly arrived shortly after the 40 day memorial service and stated to all present that he was carrying a personal message from *Rade Markovic*, the Chief of the State Security Service.

He claimed he had great news - the "message from the Chief" seemed to be encouraging, "Don't interfere in court proceedings. Don't expose anything or question the three suspects in the court room for the murder. Be calm and placid. You have a green light to eliminate all responsible for Arkan's death, but you have to be cautious and get it done without any proof or witnesses."

Green light to eliminate all responsible?

We all stared at him quite baffled, debating whether to feel sorry for this fellow or just question his basic logic and sanity. Rade Rakonjac, my father's closest confidant rightfully cussed him out and called him a traitor. The rest of us were unsure how to react because we did not believe what Pelevic was saying.

"What men again does this guy possess?" I asked my two brothers as we burst out laughing.

I quickly compared the situation with a famous event from 1944. As the Red Army pushed deeper into Poland, Churchill urgently flew to Moscow to plead with Stalin. Upon arguing that the Pope will never allow Poland to be occupied again, Stalin took a puff out of his pipe, smiled, and replied, "And how many divisions does the Pope have?"

Just the thought of Pelevic fantasizing and pretending to be a hereditary don or the head of a powerful organization was ridiculous enough to keep us laughing all day.

To this very day, it remains uncertain why Pelevic continues to declare that western intelligence services murdered my father.

26. "Body Warms Up Best with Hard Work"

On a frosty Friday in December of 1999, I was headed with my father towards the Obilic Stadium. If this sprawling complex was his "child," then the Sport Center Inge in Zvezdara was his baby!

He renamed it Young Obilic; he envisaged this location to become the largest and most efficient Talent Academy in the region. It would consist of a hotel, restaurant, half a dozen soccer fields, and a few office buildings. He constantly bragged to others that he was going to breed the "Future Maradonas" right there under everyone's noses. So proud was he of this start up enterprise that he would impatiently tour the site every morning to inspect the overall progress.

That particular morning, however, he was too consumed with various business meetings at his main office at the Obilic stadium. Suddenly, he received an emergency phone call informing him that due to the cold weather, all the workers and laborers at the Zvezdara complex had refused to work for the day and were sitting around a campfire. He was visibly furious and I decided to join him and attempt to calm him down.

His Chevy Suburban was running every red light and speeding heavily through the snowy streets of Belgrade. He was clearly enraged and kept repeating that there is no such thing as being too cold to perform your job. He explained, "In Bosnia a few years ago, it was one of the harshest winters I have ever experienced. All my units and I were freezing. Were we going to abandon our weapons and positions and sit by the campfire all day? NO."

Fifteen minutes had barely passed when we arrived at the Young Obilic Sports Complex. My father drove the SUV right next to the hotel building. There were around thirty construction workers sitting around a campfire. I knew that the collapse of discipline was one of the characteristics my father most despised.

As soon as the laborers saw my father walking out of the car, half of them got up and assumed their prior tasks.

However, he wasn't convinced, so he commanded them all in a straight line. Then in classic military fashion, he asserted, "Who do you think you are? You are cold? Well, the body warms up best with hard work! In the former wars, I stood outside in the dying cold when the temperature was far below 0 degrees. Did I nag and complain? NO! Every day, you get paid. And now you are spoiled to work because it's too cold? Everyone else works in the freezing cold, too! We can't change the weather and the climate! I don't want to hear again that you are cold! UNDERSTOOD? Now back to Work! NOW!"

On our way back home, my father shared another tale. "There is no greater misfortune then when discipline drops! Son, I had to forcefully return thousands of our Serbian troops back to the front lines so the enemy wouldn't occupy Banja Luka and other towns! And these cowards complain they can't work because they are too cold..."

It was the third time that winter that my father was without any bodyguards. I meant to ask him the reason, but I knew better – when he was in a bad mood, it was better to just stay away.

It was during this time that his assassins waited around the corner at a traffic light. They had an RPG ready to fire at him.

He was unaware that his Chevy Suburban with level five armor protection had prolonged his life for another few weeks.

The powerful persons in charge of orchestrating his murder clearly understood they needed him to be in an open space, away from his "fortress on wheels."

Another attempt on his life was to occur in front of Madera, of the most famous restaurants in the city. My father would conduct business there and dine with other high profile "persons of interest."

One night a car was strangely parked right outside of the main entrance. Nishki, one of my father's bodyguards and hardened veteran of the Yugoslav wars, quickly understood that the car was at the wrong place. The vehicle smelled like gunpowder, which only alerted him further. As he approached the driver, the car sped off. He had just saved my father's life - an attempt that would have been reminiscent of a typical Beirut assassination.

The state Security Service had been tracking his phone calls and shadowing his whereabouts for almost four months. They knew he frequented the Inter-Continental Hotel; the location of a boutique where his wife liked to shop for clothes.

The location had been chosen.

27. "But you are a Partizan Fan"

Soccer is by far the most popular sport in Serbia, largely dominated by the two biggest clubs from the capital, Partizan and Red Star. The rivalry runs so deep, that there are numerous cases of actual family members supporting the opposing teams. In that respect, Family Raznatovic was no different.

My grandfather Veljko was a proud colonel in the Yugoslav Air Force. The two clubs were both founded by the State Authorities right after The Second World War. Logically, Veljko was a Partizan sympathizer, due to the fact that most military personnel supported the "black and white" team. Red Star, on the other hand, adopted the red and white colors, and drew the core of its support from the Ministry of Internal Affairs. The rivalry on the pitch between the army and the police based teams never simmered down, and only intensified as the years passed.

As I said before, it is known that my father had a turbulent childhood. Just to spite his own father, he reversed the family tradition and began openly supporting Red Star. He went on to become leader of the massive Red Star fanatical supporters, and in 1989 accomplished in combining all the various subgroups into one massive and united front, The Delije.

So passionate was my father about Red Star, that he used to dress my brother and I constantly in red and white and bring us to Marakana stadium to watch every Red Star home game. However, he was also aware that every week when my brother and I would go to the Zemun (an adjacent city) to visit my mother's relatives, they would dress me in black and white and make me wave the massive Partizan flag they so proudly possessed. Even though I was only five at the time, my heart began to shift towards the black and white team.

The decision was finally made when my uncle took me to the famous JNA stadium to watch Partizan take on the mighty Italian giant Internazionale Milano. The atmosphere, energy, and passion I felt that day is simply indescribable. I was in such a state of nirvana that I decided to finally break the news to my father, and everyone else, that I was a die-hard Partizan fan!

A few days later, the top executive of Partizan at the time arrived to our house to pick me up and bring me to the stadium. He lavishly bombarded me with various Partizan memorabilia, jerseys, scarves, and soccer balls. This gesture further intensified the rivalry between my twin brother and I that exists to this day. At every soccer, basketball, handball, water polo, and even volleyball game, we would spot one another on the opposing side, passionately supporting our own team.

Sadly enough, the politics in Serbia have always infiltrated every aspect of society, including sports. I wondered numerous times why I had to raise three fingers in the air with the rest of the fans and shout," Svi, Svi, Svi" (Everyone, Everyone, Everyone). I was clueless to assess that the majority of Partizan fans supported Vuk Draskovic, the key opposition candidate in Serbia, while most of the Red Star fans were die hard Slobodan Milosevic supporters.

The yearly clash of the two Belgrade clubs exceeded any national holiday in terms of significance. When the Eternal Derby took place, the whole country became paralyzed. It was the most desirable day for any soccer fan in the country.

I will always remember when my brother and I rushing home from school to retrieve the tickets my father had waiting for us. As soon as he handed me the south stand ticket where all Partizan fanatical supporters gather, he turned around and informed my brother that he had a surprise for him. He reached out from a bag and handed him five flares to take to the Red Star's north stand. I waited a few minutes for my flares, but then he mockingly disclosed, "Sorry son, but you are a Partizan Fan. This privilege is only given to a Red Star supporter."

In major disbelief, I headed to the stadium. I managed to take out all my anger and frustration in the stands, where I fanatically shouted and backed my team with full force. I am still grateful to my father because of this particular act -

he only further heartened and cemented my love and passion toward my beloved team.

28."He Must Make It"

My father was present at every single soccer game in the country when his club Obilic played. He also extended his reach great lengths to assure that the forty or so fans of Obilic were not harassed or beaten by the opposing fans or the police.

I recollect one instance when my father shouted at a police officer who wouldn't allow the fans of Obilic to leave the stadium as they were getting pelted by rocks and bricks by the opposing fans.

He roared at the officer, "UNLOCK the gate and let them out! You think you are a tough shot??? Why don't you go to Kosovo and prove yourself how big your balls are! It's easy playing a tough shot here amongst the 15 year olds, wearing a badge and not giving a damn about their safety and well-being?" The uniformed police officer unlocked the gate and the fans were safely escorted. My dad made a slight pause and then continued, "I personally led to battle 2,000 police units in the fiercest assaults of the previous war, you understand?"

That moment resonated with me a while and I didn't fully grasp the significance of his words.

I personally led to battle 2,000 police units?

Well, not until the day I caught my father pacing back and forth in his office at the Obilic Stadium. He was clearly expecting an urgent phone call.

"Has it been picked up?" he would nervously inquire every ten minutes and then hang up the phone after he heard a negative response. He repeated a few times to himself, "He must make it."

After about half of an hour, one of his close lieutenants rushed in and delivered him a small box. His mood immediately brightened, and he instructed me to get in the car. He had me carefully hold the strange little box for him. I thought we were headed home, when he clearly sped past our distinguishable house.

Five minutes later we entered a heavily guarded apartment building in the elite Dedinje neighborhood. After a police officer escorted us to an apartment upstairs, an older lady opened the door and greeted my father warmly with the traditional Serbian three-time kiss on the cheek. He quickly inquired, "God Bless! Where is our patient? I brought him some revolutionary remedy!"

Upon setting our feet in, the very pale and sweaty looking older man was lying on the couch. My father was quick to lecture the wife to prop open all the windows so "the virus can't linger in the house." He then requested the box I was in charge of holding, opened it, and explained to the sick man, "I was waiting on this for two full days to arrive from Leverkusen, Germany. This is the newest, ground-breaking medicine that will exterminate the flu and clean up your body in just a few days."

Father then took one of the liquid capsules, twisted the cap and handed it over to the ill gentleman. "Don't worry, my brother, your time is not up yet. I wouldn't let anything happen to you."

Along with Milosevic's own wife and the chief of the powerful State Security Service, two of the highest ranking police chiefs, Vlajko Stoiljkovic and Dragan Ilic, were directly involved in the planning, organization, and cover-up of my father's murder.

I was too young to recognize how essential this sick man had become to my father's survival. The truth could not be simpler - he was my father's only ally left in the entire police force! All of his prominent friends were dismissed from their powerful posts. Some of them were brutally murdered.

I will not disclose the name of this official, but I will admit - I was unaware for a long time who he was.

A few years later, I was watching television when I recognized a familiar face standing on trial before the Hague Tribunal for his involvement in the Yugoslav wars.

I instantly recognized him. It was the patient whose medicine I was entrusted to carry.

29. The Serbian Dream

Every time my brother and I would attempt to inquire further into our father's past, he would always provide the same staunch answer, "Son, don't ever ask me what I did when I was young."

My brother and I constantly bugged him to confirm if a given rumor we had heard about him was true or not. On one occasion, I couldn't hold back and simply had to hear the complete tale. I summoned enough courage and brought up a story about him robbing a bank back in Sweden in the 1970s. Rumor was he gifted the beautiful teller with a red rose. He instantly chuckled, then warned me never to inquire about his past again.

When I arrived in Belgrade in summer 1999, my father eagerly took me to the Obilic Stadium to proudly display the recently finished stand on the eastern part of the pitch. He boasted how Obilic would possess the most modern and beautiful stadium in the world. He simply could not stop fantasizing about his grand project. When he realized I paid little attention, he turned toward me and demanded to know, "Son, where do you see yourself in ten, twenty years?" "I would like to be a lawyer or perhaps the mayor of Belgrade," I reasoned.

"You have to understand one thing son," he reckoned, "I never had an opportunity to have another path in life like you have. The times were very different back in the day. That's why I have unfortunately spent more time abroad than I did here at home."

As we strolled past the soccer pitch, he walked straight toward the very center and continued, "Your father wants you to finish school, perhaps a prestigious university, and never to draw yourself in the same path that I took in life."

"Don't worry, I don't even desire to," I replied.

"Son, I know we are faithful patriots, and it runs deep in our blood. I have defended this land with a rifle, but you might be called to serve your country in an entirely different way." "Of course," I replied, pretending I knew what he was trying to convey.

"Have you heard of John Lennon?" he fired back. "Well, he said famously 'these times, they are changing'."

I just nodded my head. He pondered for a few seconds, then turned towards me and softly spoke, "Let me tell you, Son. I long for the day when I will see you defend this land with a pen and a briefcase...then your father will be really proud of you." "I will do my best," I reassured him.

"Son, the Greatest thing you can do in life is to be the in the service of your people. We Serbs have been fighting for a thousand years for only one thing – *survival*," he reasoned, "We live in such a hostile neighborhood, surrounded by enemies on all sides who cherish the moment Serbia becomes weak so they can devour us. That's why it is our holy duty to assure our homeland survives another 1,000 years, and every Serb must sacrifice and equally contribute one way or another to ensure this *Serbian Dream* becomes a reality."

Suddenly, his phone rang and he answered. It was Zoran Uskokovic Skole, informing him that he was waiting to meet him outside of his office.

"Let's walk back to the office. I gotta meet with Skole to go over some stuff."

So what exactly happened between Skole and my father? The story goes that two months before my father's assassination, Skole had suddenly appeared in front of our house in Belgrade. He demanded a million German marks for bringing a star player to Obilic and threatened he wouldn't leave until he got his money. My stepmother immediately phoned my father.

Ten minutes later, my father showed up, and instantly began slapping Skole before he ran to his car and took off. He quickly escaped to Hungary where he would reside until my father was murdered. Nobody realized that this was all a plot by the State Security to turn Skole away from my father in order to utilize Skole's thugs.

Skole was guaranteed his criminal gang would become the most powerful clan in the country. (He was also eyeing millions of dollars of future transfer funds for a star player who he rumored to have brought to Obilic.) However, by agreeing to directly carry out the plot to eliminate my father, he unknowingly signed a death sentence for himself.

His involvement was immediately discovered after my father was murdered.

It is a mystery how soon Skole understood he was being tricked by the State Security. He must have realized his time was up as he watched all the men in his inner circle killed one by one.

A famed Serbian proverb states:

He who for someone digs a hole, into it himself will fall.

30. Beijing Calling

Some behavioral scientists argue that a mother possesses a miraculous instinct that naturally triggers when her child is in danger. I was always skeptical of such studies, but one instance changed my whole perception.

Every year, on the first of January, it had become a tradition for the entire family to get together and enjoy a buffet-style feast at the acclaimed InterContinental Hotel in Belgrade. This year was more special, mainly because Anastasija had been the newest addition to our already rapidly expanding family. The year was also 2000, which brought world-wide euphoria and uncertainty across the globe.

Four fully packed SUVs left the house on Ljutice Bogdana street and sped towards the Gazela onramp to merge onto the highway. The first two vehicles were filled with family members and children, and the remaining two with a half dozen security personnel. When we finally reached our destination a quarter of an hour later, I noticed a close family friend Manda greeting us in the lobby. I also noticed a familiar face, Jorga, greeting my father (along with two other men who I recognized in the paper a few weeks later when the names of my father's assassins were finally revealed).

Two hours later, after everyone was finished with their meals, our family returned back to the house. I spent the rest of the day hanging out with friends and reading comic books. I prepared myself for bed and connected my cellular phone to a charger.

Within a ten minute timespan, I had received dozen or so calls from a very puzzling number. When the cellular device finally rang again, I decided to pick up out of mere annoyance. I recognized my mother's frantic and overwrought voice, "Voka, are you all alright?" "Uhhh, yes Mama, what's the matter?"

"Nothing, I just had a really terrible feeling something happened so I had to call and make sure you are all alright."

"Of course we are OK. Anyways, how's Beijing? Did you buy me one of those Mao army hats with the red star on it?"

"Not yet. I will. Go back to bed. I was just really worried."

Three weeks later, a day after we buried my father, a very reliable and trustworthy close family friend who was employed by the State Security Service, reluctantly revealed to us, "You kids are all lucky to be alive. On the first of January, when you all went to InterContinental for your family gathering, you are so blessed that your father brought along a substantial security team to guard you."

We all stared at him quite puzzled as he continued with his finding, "We received information they weren't only going to kill your father on that day, but all you sons and even the rest of the family."

He stopped for a brief second, looked at my brother and me, and then repeated, "It was supposed to be a horrid blood bath of the entire Raznatovic family. You guys are very fortunate your father had enough security personnel with him that day because they were ready and they waited for you all."

Fourteen days later, they managed to achieve part of that plan.

31."But guys... You took the bus here"

This is one of the stories my father openly talked about. I still get approached by people from time to time inquiring about the authenticity of this acclaimed occurrence.

My father received a phone call one morning from a childhood friend who he hadn't been in contact with for years. The man apologized for the abrupt phone call and pleaded that the reason he called, with great embarrassment, was due to the simple fact that he was in deep trouble and he feared for his life. He explained that he was the owner of a very successful restaurant right off of the prominent Ibar Highway. He broke into tears when he admitted that he's been forced to pay a monthly "protection" sum to local criminals and gangsters. He claimed the month was slow for the business and the racketeers had increased their fee by 10 percent. He was worried they were going to kill him if he didn't provide the necessary funds.

"When do the thugs come to collect"? my father asked. "On the first... which means in three days, his friend sheepishly replied.

"I will be there. Don't worry. I give you my word. Everything will be taken care of."

So the first arrived, and the four thugs dropped by the restaurant to collect their "debt." The owner greeted them warmly, and suggested they proceed to the back booth. Upon realizing who was seated at the table, the four men froze without saying a word.

"Please, have a seat. There is room for everyone," my father remarked.

Puzzled and anxious, the thugs sat down. After offering them a drink, my father explained the long standing friendship he cherished with the owner of the restaurant. He then began lecturing the four frightened fellas on how it is utmost immoral and cowardly to extract fees from an honest and hardworking family man.

Startled and disturbed, the four men immediately began to apologize. They pleaded how they never knew it was his close friend and how they would never disrespect the long standing friendship between them. They begged for forgiveness and implored they would never pay this restaurant a visit again.

"That's what I like to hear!" my father exclaimed. "Now get up and go apologize to my friend for this immoral and blasphemous gesture! Inform him that he will be justly compensated for this unfair wrongdoing."

The four petrified gangsters got up, apologized to the owner, and shook his hand. They wondered if they were dismissed, and my father gave them a nod. He wished them good luck and thanked them for their understanding and cooperation.

After a mere few minutes, the four returned to the restaurant, looking severely unsettled and distressed.

"Mister Arkan," one of them pleaded, "our newest Benz has disappeared from the parking lot"

My father smirked, looked at them, and replied, "But guys ...you took the bus here."

The thugs quickly got the message and swiftly ran out, fearing for their lives.

Just as my father had predicted, the owner was justly compensated.

32."Who is this Grandma Here?"

My father was married three times in his life. He brazenly boasted that he was the proud father of nine children. Michael was the first, born in Sweden in 1975. My father was married a few years to his mother, Agneta. The next child, Sofia, born in 1977, was conceived in one of the Belgian prisons where my father was serving a sentence. Angela was the next child born in 1980; her mother was a well-known actress.

He married my mother, Natalija, in 1981 and soon after, the following year, my sister Milena was born. Ten months later, my brother and I, his two twin boys, came out of the womb. Seven years later, in 1990, my sister Masha was born.

He married Ceca in 1995 and as early as the next year, my brother Veljko was born. Anastasija, the newest addition to our sprawling family, arrived six months before his death, in May of 1999.

All the siblings knew each other pretty well. All the children resided in Belgrade, apart from Sofia who lived in Belgium, and my immediate siblings who lived in Greece. However, we would frequently visit Serbia from Athens every summer and winter holiday. Therefore, most of my dad's children would be together during this time of the year. Sofia was the only child missing, and none of us had met her yet.

Until sometime in 1998, that is. We were all relaxing in our sprawling home when my stepmother shouted from downstairs to immediately meet in our cafe, situated right next to our house. My brother and I quickly arrived and she introduced us to a younger looking lady who had similar facial features as our father.

"This is your older sister, Sofia," Ceca revealed. "Doesn't she look like a Raznatovic?"

Well that's awkward.

My brother and I stood in disbelief for a moment, then began communicating with her in English. I noticed an elderly woman seated behind her talking to my father. I turned towards Ceca and asked, "Who is this grandma here"?

Upon hearing my inquiry, Ceca, her sister, and my father all began to chuckle. The situation became uncomfortable when Sofia wondered what the laughter was all about. When I finally explained, she began tittering awkwardly and answered that the older lady was her mother.

That same night, Ceca went on to explain how my father was in jail for many months in Belgium, and Sofia's mother was one of the social workers who happened to be employed by the state to assist the inmates. She was roughly twenty years my father's senior. Regardless of the substantial gap, my father, charming that he was and not being in a woman's presence for a quite some time, quickly conquered her heart in one of their one-on-one sessions. I guess the temptation was too great to resist at the given moment.

Poor Sofia did not know who her real father was until she was twenty years old. My aunt had contacted her mother to inform her that her real father wanted to see her. Sofia's stepfather, who believed for the past two decades he was the real father of this child, took the news dreadfully.

He committed suicide the very next day.

33. Casino London

Every Sunday, my brother and I would venture out to our barge on the Sava and bask in the river with friends. We would usually end up staying there until the early evening hours, then catch a public bus to downtown Belgrade and walk around. The evening was pleasant on this lovely August day, so we decided to get off the bus at the Slavija stop, and stroll through the Terazije Boulevard which leads directly to the very center of Belgrade.

We recklessly crossed the busy Knez Milos street, and ended up right in front of Casino London. We were laughing how we jaywalked and almost got hit by a vehicle when a random voice cursed right at us, "What's so fucking funny, you little shit? You almost got hit by a car!"

Thinking it was a police officer attempting to scold a bunch of teenagers, we turned around and spotted a short, bulky man sitting outside with four large security guards. Our teenage entourage stood still in amazement and disbelief at the rudeness of these five lads.

"What the fuck are you looking at kid?" the pudgy man exclaimed. "We just want to let you know that you are being out of line, Sir," I replied. "Who cares if a bunch of us cross the street. It should be none of your business."

"Get the fuck outta here, you little shit," he asserted.

"Our father is a godfather to the owner of this casino, and you should show a bit more courtesy and respect," my brother fired back."

The pudgy man suddenly got up, shadowed by the four gorillas. When he got in my brother's face and openly declared that he doesn't "give a fuck" who our father is, my brother kicked him right in the head, and the stout man fell on the ground. The four bodyguards rushed towards my brother, and one swung his fist toward him, but luckily my brother was quick so he only got a scratch on the nose. I happened to catch a glimpse of their pistols around their waists, and cried out to my brother to run as fast as he could, knowing he was an athlete and they would have a hard time keeping up with his sprint.

The anticipation was nerve racking while the two of them ran after him and disappeared half a mile away. I quickly called my father and informed him of the situation, begging him to call Wolf and immediately defuse the situation before someone got severely hurt.

"Don't tell me they charged at you 15 year olds?" he presumed. "Yes Dad," I remarked, "We would have fought them if they carried no guns." "Stay right there. I am coming right now."

A few minutes later, the casino manager burst out holding his head in incredulity and disbelief. He began shouting at the pudgy man and the guards, "You idiots! What have you done? You are all dead! Do you know who you just attacked? Arkan's twin boys! He just raged at Wolf warning him if something happened to his boys he will hold everyone accountable."

The pudgy man who started this whole scenario in the first place walked up to us and began apologizing and claiming he never wanted to hurt or disrespect us, and that he was only joking. I calmly told them that I accepted his apology, but I'm not the one they should be apologizing to.

Just as the tense situation cooled down, you could hear the sound of screeching tires turning from a hundred yards away. My father's Chevy, followed by another black SUV, climbed on the sidewalk and drove straight into the entrance of the Casino. He got out of the car and yelled, "Where are my sons?" After realizing that my brother had a cut on his nose, he went berserk. He started slapping the four security guards who attacked us and who chased my brother. He kept yelling as he was slapping them, "You pussies! They are 15 years old! You think it's brave to attack children? Are you a big shot now?"

He lined them all up in a straight line, demanding to know which one of them charged at my brother. But in the nick of time, the casino manager re-appeared with the short, bulky man. He pleaded with my dad that this was all a misunderstanding. The bulky man explained that he is the "head security" and rightfully interjected, "Commandant, please don't. It was all me."

"What do you mean", my father seemed puzzled. "This is my entire fault. I am responsible for starting this whole mess. Please leave my men alone."

"Oh, so you are the one who put my twin boys in danger? Well you come with me."

After a few minutes I ran downstairs to attempt to calm my father down. "Hear me out now. You are lucky Wolf and I are godfathers. Go to the nearest church now and light a candle for him because he saved your life. If anyone EVER puts my twin boys in danger, he will never be found again! Do you understand? Now get outta here! QUICKLY!"

34."We will always help the poor"

"Whoever is generous to the poor lends to the Lord, and he will repay him for his deed" - Proverbs 19:17

Despite all of his flaws and negative characteristics that are greatly speculated and discussed in the media, little is known to this very day about one of my father's greatest and most sincere causes.

The Birth of Christ is the second most meaningful day in our faith, falling only behind Easter in importance. Every Christmas Eve, my father would gather his entire family and head to the local church in order to attend liturgy. He was a devout Christian Orthodox, and I recollect how he would prepare for this occasion by stuffing his pockets with giant stacks of cash.

Giving to the needy.

My father took great satisfaction in this generous act. St.Nicholas was our family's Saint Protector. So humble and modest was this extraordinary person that he spent his entire life in the service of the needy. (The very concept of Santa Claus giving presents to children was mimicked after his gracious deeds).

A well-known orphanage was located in close proximity to the church. These poor souls knew that my father had arrived to that church every Christmas Eve, so many of them customarily waited every year for my father to arrive. However, as the years passed, their ranks seemed to be swelling with the marginalized Roma children, who eagerly arrived from all areas of town in order to reap the fruits of this benevolent act.

Year after year, we would witness the same euphoria and jubilation as my dad's signature Chevrolet appeared in front of the church. He was not be able to open his car door because he would get swarmed by the orphans requesting money. As soon as he stepped out, he quickly grabbed his giant stacks of cash and began handing out the money.

"God bless you, Arkan!" a young gypsy boy yelled after he received his donation. "Now I can buy a new soccer ball," another cried. "I am going to buy a Barbie doll," a little girl murmured.

As he was getting swamped from all sides, he quickly turned toward my brothers and me and demanded we provide a helping hand, "Take out the other stacks and start handing it out. These are all our children."

I recognized how the bleak and dismal faces of these kids instantly lit up with happiness and joy as soon as he handed them some cash. My father smiled genuinely, watching these destitute and bleak souls jump with delight.

However, so carried away was he with this gesture that when we walked inside the church he was left with no cash to pay for the candles. He turned toward his wife and asked how much cash she had in her purse. He even requested we give all the money we had in our pockets so he could "tip" the priests and pay for the candles.

On our way home, he began lecturing me and my brother, "Let me explain something to you - We must always help the poor. Don't worry, God will give you tenfold in return!" "We know that. You say that every year, Dad," I reasoned. "It is the moral duty of every man. For example, in all major religions - Christianity, Judaism, and Islam you are required to help the poor and the needy."

He paused for a few seconds and then loudly affirmed, "We will always help the poor. The Raznatovic family has always played our part. What good is it if we are servants of our country if we don't help the marginalized ones? It is one of the greatest deeds a man can do. That's why you need to make it your mission in life to always fulfill this requirement."

I was not aware how dedicated my father was to this statement when he was alive. However, to this very day, I still get messages and emails from people who express gratitude and appreciation for my dad's benevolent deeds. Commitment to social justice has always played a distinctive role in my life.

In 1995, my father founded a foundation called TRECE DETE (THIRD CHILD), which provided financial as well as material assistance in food, clothing, and school supplies to poor families having more than two children. The purpose was to tackle poverty as well as help parents to expand their families. It is unfortunate that the foundation has been terminated for more than fifteen years.

The politicians in Serbia who rise to power continuously choose to ignore the critical needs of these unfortunate souls. They don't recognize that the most pristine struggle one can wage in life is war against poverty.

I am greatly honored to announce that it will be my utmost priority to fully re-activate the Third Child Foundation. We will not launch this endeavor because we want to, but because we care and have always dauntlessly believed in this sacred cause.

We will always help the poor!

35. "Nobody will steal in my name"

One of the deeds my father most detested was when a member of his paramilitary force would steal and racketeer in his name. He would strictly punish the perpetrator and set an example to all, but there was always a greedy and voracious individual who aspired to get away with this disgraceful and unspeakable crime.

I remember this specific incident occurred in the summer of 1997. I was headed home from the Partizan-Kroacija soccer match, when my brother urgently phoned and requested to meet me immediately outside of the Avala restaurant by our house.

When I arrived there, Nikola explained how Milan, one of our favorite sentries guarding the house, was locked up in a cage in our parking lot. He further clarified that he was well guarded by three other guards and that nobody was to venture near the cage or speak with the accused until father returned home from Zitoradja, his wife's village in southern Serbia. These were direct orders from our father.

When curiosity reached its peak, my brother and I secretly attempted to reach the cage without being seen. One of the head guards approached us quickly and explained the directive given by our father. We demanded to know the reason he was in the cage, and the answer was swift, "An elderly woman stopped by to ask if we still have the detective agency available for hire. Milan was the sentry outside of the house here, so he introduced himself as Toma, and told her that our prices had gone up because we always get the job done. She needed help in recovering her son's stolen vehicle and he told her the service was going to cost her three thousand dollars. Poor lady arrived here today, frightened, demanding to speak with Toma! She began apologizing and crying because she couldn't come up with the third thousand dollar installment, but pleaded that she had put up her apartment for sale and needed more time to come up with the money. After she was finished, I explained to her that there was no Toma here and we didn't provide any detective work since last year. When she explained what he looked like, I knew exactly who he was. I called the Komandant, and he gave me strict orders to lock him up and not let anyone near him until he gets here."

My brother and I could not go to bed that night. We kept looking outside of the window for when our father would return home, so we could witness how the drama would unfold. Knowing our father well, we knew the con man's fate was pretty much sealed.

When our father returned home, we spotted the guards bringing the accused downstairs in the patio in front of our main house door.

I don't recollect seeing my father so enraged! He started slapping him and punching him in the face while cursing at him incessantly and reminding him how he humiliated and shamed the whole Guard's name as well as my father's.

"Nobody will steal in my name, you understand!" my father yelled, "The Guard's reputation has always been to protect the good and honest people, not to scam and rob them."

He then pulled out a hockey stick from storage and started beating him so severely that my brother and I had to run and get a bucket of water in order for the scammer to regain his consciousness. The accused kept pleading for my father to stop, which only further infuriated him and my father started kicking his face with his pointed shoes while he thundered at him, "Shame on you! Poor lady comes seeking help from us, and you take her money, bring shame to my name and my guard? We are the Serbian Army. A Serbian soldier never steals or scams others, you hear me?"

While kicking him everywhere, the con-man lost consciousness again.

Another bucket of water.

I will never forget the man's purple, bloody, swollen face, nor his sorrowful stare at my brother and me right before the police cruiser arrived and apprehended him.

Just in case you are wondering what happened with the poor lady? My father met with her the very next day, apologized wholeheartedly, and returned the full sum of money that the scammer extracted from her. With the assistance from his connections in the streets and the police, her son's vehicle was recovered and returned to her within the following 24 hours.

36. "Arkan father, Jokso godfather*"

My father returned to Yugoslavia at the beginning of the 80s from his "duties abroad." He was astonished how rapidly his beloved city was changing and the thought of settling and residing there for good greatly excited him.

Belgrade was undergoing a massive transformation at this time. Tourists kept pouring in as this regional hub seemed more appealing than ever to foreign investment. The Gasterbeiters (as Yugoslav expatriates were called who lived abroad) began massively arriving back home now that Tito's iron hand had vanished. It was around this time that my father cemented deep friendships with some of the most iconic people of the city - Darko Asanin, Slavko Mijovic, Rako Stanisic, Djordje Bozovic, Dragan Malesevic, Milan Djordjevic, and Dragan Joksovic (amongst others). They were all well known in the social circles, where their honorable and chivalrous codes of conduct greatly enhanced their reputations and set an everlasting guidance to a younger generation of dreamers.

By the year 1996, Belgrade had become a gloomy and isolated city in Eastern Europe. Years of sanctions and wars in neighboring regions had seriously squeezed the vibrant energy and life out of the once bustling and booming metropolis.

August is a hot month in Belgrade. I had just returned from the Atlanta Olympic Games with my older brother, Mihajlo. One night, Mihajlo informed me to get ready because "Jokso" is waiting for us at the Alexander Palace hotel in downtown Belgrade and we have to go see him. "Who is Jokso?" I wondered. "What our father is in Serbia," Michael explained, "Jokso is in Sweden."

As we entered this posh hotel, a loud voice excitedly greeted us in the lobby. I had never seen a more frightening man in my life. He had to be at least two meters tall (6 foot 6), with absolutely the broadest set of shoulders and chest of any man I knew.

After politely informing the two ladies in his company that it was time to sit with friends, they immediately excused themselves and departed. My brother and he began exchanging various stories about their mutual friends in Sweden. I took a great interest in the conversation when he mentioned a race track in Stockholm.

"Jokso, you own a race track?" I interrupted. "Yes kiddo," he replied. "Wow! That's so cool! I love betting money and watch horses race," I admitted.

"Well I tell you what: you can come to Stockholm to visit whenever you want and I will take you to my racetrack and show you around. You can also ride any horse you want."

When we met our father at Hotel Jugoslavija the next day, he demanded I urgently pick a Godfather so I can get baptized. He had been pushing me for a week to choose somebody, claiming it was embarrassing I was a Raznatovic and not baptized in the church yet. I immediately declared that I wanted Jokso to be my Godfather. Michael and my father were simply overjoyed with my choice.

The Christening took place the very next day at the church by the JNA Stadium. Around 30 people attended, and after the ceremony the whole entourage relocated to the iconic Avala restaurant by our house. After everyone saluted to my health and began feasting, my father turned towards me and loudly stated, "Son, remember this, you are a lucky guy. You now have Arkan as your father, and Jokso as your Godfather. Nobody is in better hands than you, son."

Regrettably, my father's statement proved to be valid for a very short period of time. Jokso was murdered inside one of his racetracks in Stockholm a year and a half later on February 4, 1998.

Twenty three months later, my father was assassinated.

37."God - Give Me Bayern"!

Football Club Obilic had become my father's ultimate fixation in the latter half of the 1990s. He would spend all day in his office at the Vracar Stadium conducting the club's daily operations. During the weekends, if his club played a home game, he would spend all day in his office and then casually slip down to the stands.

In 1998, Obilic became the champion of Yugoslavia. It was a considerable shock to all, due to the fact that for the first time since the dissolution of the former Yugoslavia, a small club had curtailed the dominance of the two local giants, Partizan and Red Star.

One of the greatest benefits in capturing the national title was the opportunity to qualify for the next year's Uefa Champions League, where Europe's top seeded clubs competed for continental dominance. This famed competition fueled massive amounts of money for every team that qualified. My father was also eager to build a name for Obilic, and the opportunity seemed quite golden.

The day the European Football Association's highest body convened to draw all the teams competing in the prestigious competition, my brother and I were in my father's office. There were at least thirty people around us eagerly waiting to witness who would be Obilic's next opponent. We glanced at my father sitting at his desk, with an icon in his head. His prayers were loudly repeated, "God, Give me Bayern! Please give me Bayern!" We were all a bit perplexed, due to the fact that legendary Bayern Munich, one of the most successful European Clubs, possessed one of the strongest teams in Europe. Roughly half of Germany's National Soccer Team played for this Bavarian giant!

But why would he want to face Bayern so badly?

My father was prompt to explain, "When we kick them out of the competition, the whole world will hear about a brave little Obilic! We are going to become one of the most popular clubs in Europe in a heartbeat."

My brother and I skeptically glanced at one another. We knew our father was an immense optimist with towering self-confidence. Reality is however differing, and we knew that the quality of players his club possessed would stand no chance against the Bayern squad. After all, how possibly could the players of Obilic, who only recently played in third and fourth regional leagues in Serbia, compete against the distinguished German "Blitzkrieg Football Machine"?

Nevertheless, God answered his prayer and indeed paired him with Bayern. My father could not believe it! He was so thrilled and adrenalized that he kept running and jumping around the office like a little kid getting his favorite toy. He declared he couldn't wait for Goliath to feel David's slingshot!

The epilogue is quite clear to all. Sure Obilic players were brave and put up a fierce fight, but they were simply no match for the Bavarian Steamroller. Obilic got demolished by four goals in Munich, but managed to draw the second game in Belgrade. My father was proud of his boys, but blamed the coach for the humiliating defeat in Munich.

Following his club's elimination, my father famously stated, "It doesn't matter, we are patient. We'll take the Champions League title next year."

To describe how powerful Bayern Munich was that year, they swept all the teams in their path and reached the final title game. They were winning against the famed Manchester United until the very last minutes of the game, when the English club managed to score two goals in injury time and claim the European title.

38. Rendezvous with Misha

Misha was one of the top commanders in my father's paramilitary unit and like a second father to my brother and I. We dearly loved and respected him, and he even took time to visit us in Greece while he was on a honeymoon with his wife.

When the Tigers were officially disbanded in 1996, my brother and I noticed him around our father less. Every time we would inquire about his whereabouts, the answer was the same, "Misha works for the state now. He is busy battling terrorists in Kosovo."

When our father was murdered, Misha was one of the first ones to arrive at our house to express condolences. A few hours after our father was properly buried, he gathered my brother and me for a necessary chat, "Listen twins, you are like my sons and you need to promise me to stay away from Serbia for the next ten years! Things are very heated right now, and until we get them back on track, I cannot have you two lingering around."

After solemnly swearing we wouldn't be coming back for a while, somehow the patriotic fervor swept our hearts, and my brother Nikola and I were headed back to Serbia in complete confidentiality. We simply lied to our mother that we were going to Mykonos Island to find jobs for the summer. In order not to arouse any suspicion, I was forced to use my somewhat extraordinary acting capabilities and phoned my mother every day to brag how beautiful the island was.

I was sitting one day in the Kalemegdan fortress in Belgrade sipping on a cola, when I rang my mother, "Mom, you were so right! Mykonos is amazing! White sandy beaches, pristine and pure sea, clean as a tear..."
"I told you!" she exclaimed, "But you never listened.
"Nikola, stop splashing me with sea water!" I recoiled. "Tell him Mom, he's gonna get my phone wet."

We were laughing and getting a kick out of my flawless performance for a few days before we were spotted somewhere in the city and the word reached our mother. She kept denying we were in Serbia, and claimed we were working on the islands and kept in touch with her every day.

We are still not sure who exactly convinced her that we were spotted, but when she called my Greek cell phone, due to roaming rules, an answering machine from the Serbian Telecommunications Company informed her in Serbian that the mobile customer was unavailable. Our cover had definitely been blown.

She went on a rampage and quickly phoned the only person who still possessed authority over us - Misha. He called my cell phone and demanded we remain inside our friend's apartment until he "[sent] a vehicle to pick us up." Phone calls came pouring in from our loyal people attempting to frighten us how Misha is extremely livid and how he might teach us a lesson with a few hard slaps on the face.

Shortly, the vehicle arrived with four men wearing bulletproof vests to escort us to the meeting with Misha. We tried communicating with them as the vehicle sped dauntlessly through the streets of Belgrade, but no man in the vehicle responded with a single word.

They are trying to scare us.

Barely ten minutes had passed, when the vehicle halted in front of a deserted establishment. As we strolled in, I realized there was no single guest inside except Misha. He was sitting alone in one of the booths, evidently frustrated.

We could sense he was glad to see us, but we understood he needed to play the strict guardian role as well. He was clearly disappointed we broke the promise given to him. He rightfully vexed his anger, "You fuck ups! Didn't we all agree that you would stay away from this country for ten years? You don't realize the gravity of the situation and obviously you two clearly don't give a fuck!"

He suddenly stopped when the waitress arrived to take a drink order. As soon as she left our presence, he continued in a more coherent tone, "You have to understand, the two of you are his twin boys, his sons. You are always going to be enemies number one to these thugs and haters because they know when you mature, you will be seeking vengeance for your father's death. That said, don't be stupid again, just stay out and let professionals do their job."

He took a moment to sip on his Red Bull, and then concluded, "Your train departs for Athens at seven in the morning and you better be on it. I am serious."

So the following morning, my brother and I were in the train headed back to Greece. We knew we were about to undergo our mother's wrath and fury as soon as we got off the train, but we simply couldn't stop laughing about it.

As our father always remarked, "You do foolish stuff when you're young."

39."I will be the Champion of Yugoslavia"

Throughout his life, my father never hid his infatuation for European Football (soccer). So deeply was he infatuated with this sport that he finally decided in 1994 to purchase a football club and become an owner.

The name of the club was FK Pristina, and it was located in the capital of the turbulent Serbian province of Kosovo. The club was performing well in the second national division, but my father found it quite strenuous having to journey down to Pristina every week. He searched for a new club to purchase closer to home.

The opportunity finally arrived a year later when a third division club from the suburb of Vracar entered the Second Division. The name of the Club was Obilic, named after a Serbian folk hero who notoriously murdered the Ottoman Sultan in a famed battle in 1389. The club's stadium consisted of a football pitch surrounded by four fences and an old, tattered house which acted as a changing room for the players. The club was on sale due to financial troubles.

This is it!

So after purchasing the club, my father worked round the clock to recruit new players, staff, and a fan base. He began investing the majority of his finances in expanding the stadium and constructing brand new stands. He managed to attract the top talented players from lower leagues, and soon became a force to be reckoned with. At the end of the year, Obilic was first in the second league and the following summer joined the highest Yugoslav league.

My father was tremendously jubilant upon entering premier competition. He openly bragged that the "unmerited domination of Red Star and Partizan had finally come to an abrupt end." One of the owners of another prominent club in the highest league overheard my father openly boasting about his title ambitions and decided to challenge him, "You know Arkan, there is no way the state would ever let you be the champion!"

"You clearly forget that I am Arkan!" my father bragged, "I can't believe out of all people you underestimate me. Would you care to make it interesting?"

"There is simply no way you will be ahead of Red Star and Partizan." "I bet you one hundred thousand dollars I will be the Champion of Yugoslavia this year!"

"Deal," smirked his colleague as they shook hands, "but we both know they'll never allow it."

Nine months later, Obilic became the first team since the creation of the new Yugoslav Federation to wrestle the title away from the two Belgrade Giants. The following day, my father was one hundred thousand dollars richer.

I told you I would be the Champion of Yugoslavia.

40. " That's just me revenging Arkan"

Zoran Uskokovic Skole was killed on the 27th of April, 2000. From the moment he began to flee the vehicles firing bullets at him, the whole episode mimicked a fast paced scene from a high budget Hollywood action movie. The city-wide hunt lasted for approximately half an hour before his "Audi" was sprayed with endless bullets.

The conflict between Skole and my father exploded a few months before my father was murmured. The fact remains that my father slapped him and the rationale behind was that Skole openly demanded a million dollars from the future transfer of Nikola Lazetic, the key player of in my father's soccer club. The other possible purpose for their discord is believed to be the unmannerly way Skole was caught staring at my stepmother's cleavage (this was only a rumor). One thing remains for certain - one of these two reasons, if not both, had caused my father to instantly confront him with a few slaps. Skole was forced to leave the country, fearing for his life.

We were all informed the next day after my father's assassination that it was Skole's men who directly carried out the murder. However, the planning, support, logistics, and the complete post cover-up of the murder scene further revealed that it was a clandestine operation which involved the highest level of professional state operatives. It was obvious to everyone that a few criminal thugs had no capacity or ability to complete such a risky endeavor on their own.

Roughly two months had passed following my father's execution, when Skole's gang and his inner circle began to get murdered one by one.

On March 21st, Skole's close friend and business partner Branislav Lainovic Dugi was murdered in Belgrade. Shortly before he was killed, he notably criticized my father in a highly circulated newspaper.

Two days later, Zoran Davidovic Canda was killed on the freeway returning to Belgrade from Dugi's funeral in Novi

Sad. Canda was a well-known local gangster and Skole's right hand man.

A month passed when Skole was finally executed along with his bodyguard (who happened to be working for the Ministry of the Interior (police). This most recent salvo of murders on the streets of Belgrade sparked a great deal of outrage in the Serbian press. It proved to be a total embarrassment and lack of ability of the State to guarantee safety and stability.

The Minister of the interior was Vlajko Stoiljkovic; the civilian head of the entire police force and directly involved in my father's murder. The story goes he furiously summoned Jerry, one of his high ranking operatives who was very close to my father. He furiously demanded, "Tell me what's going on in my town? Where are all these murders coming from?"

Jerry just stood composed, tapped him on the shoulder, and reassuringly whispered in his ear, "Don't worry, Pops... that's just me avenging Arkan!"

41. "Israel is our Greatest Friend"

The year was 1993 and the war in Bosnia was already raging to the full extent. Bosnian Serbs clashed with Bosnian Muslims, and Bosnian Croatians also joined the fray and clashed severely with the Bosnian Muslims for the control of Herzegovina.

My father had been away to the "front" for the majority of the days of the year. I missed my father, so at times if he didn't return to Belgrade, I would catch a ride in one of his guard's signature Mitsubishi Pajero SUVs and head to Erdut, his guard's main base in Slavonia, Croatia.

What seemed different on this occasion was that two strange looking foreigners were sitting at our cafe by our house sipping on espressos and waiting to board the SUV that would transport us to Erdut. They were always watched and guarded by Vule, my father's trusted security chief for Belgrade, along with a few other Tigers. I tried inquiring to who these two gentlemen were, and was told only that they were from Israel's Defense Forces, and they were VIP guests who my father had been expecting.

I tried hard to communicate with them in my broken French and English, but to no avail. I recollect the older gentleman turning toward me, shaking my hand and exclaiming – "Serbia and Israel - friends." I had never heard of this country of Israel, even though my grandma had mentioned that the people of their faith were holed up with her in a concentration camp during WWII.

Upon our arrival, the whole Serbian Volunteer Guard was transformed into the guard of honor. The Israeli friends were saluted, and then led to the distinguished officer's canteen, where kosher lunch was made for them and the whole officer corps. I had never seen my father treat anybody this highly, not even the high ranking officials from Serbia, the JNA, or the self-proclaimed Republic of Serbian Krajina's officials.

Upon completion of the day, I was watching a movie in my father's room in the barracks. It was late in the hour when he walked in visibly exhausted and asked me if I would be willing to join them the following day in an expedition to Vukovar. I declined the offer, simply because it was one of the most frightful sights I had ever witnessed. Nevertheless, I was curious to find out who these Israelis were and why they were given such royal treatment throughout the day.

Upon which my father clarified, "Son, you have to know that we have no true friends. The Croatians are supported by the Vatican, Germany, and other Western States. The Bosnian Muslims are supported by Iran and all the Islamic countries who funnel money and weapons to them. We are left to fight alone for our Orthodox Faith and our people."

"What About Russia, Dad, they are going to help us, right?"

"No Sun, unfortunately, President Yeltsin is very weak, and although he keeps promising us weapons and money, all he has sent us are medical supplies. Even some that expired last year and we had to throw them away. I long for the day when a strong leader becomes Russia's president so he can transform our brotherly Russia into a superpower again."

"So we are all alone then," I realized. "Well Son, we get some important financial assistance and volunteers from Greece. But this is why you saw the two gentlemen from the Israeli Armed forces. They understand our position, because their people are in the same situation - surrounded by hostile enemies on all sides whose only goal is to exterminate them from this world. This is why we have established a lasting military cooperation with them. The weapons and intelligence we get from them allows us to fight in this war and effectively defend ourselves. This is why at the moment, Israel is our greatest friend."

The fruitful relationship did not end just as the Bosnian War concluded in 1996. When my high school varsity soccer team was invited to compete in the International Tournament in Tel Aviv, I had to go to the Israeli embassy in Athens and apply for a visa to enter the Jewish state. My father had already pulled his strings, and the clearance arrived directly from Tel Aviv.

My visa was immediately approved.

42."I don't care if they are Arkan's sons"...

My hometown of Athens hosted the European Basketball Tournament in the summer of 1995. After years of embargo and sanctions, the resurgence of the Yugoslav National Basketball Team was finally witnessed by all. The euphoria amongst all Serbian Nationals residing in Greece was so immense that all available tickets for the games were completely sold out!

My brother and I, tremendous fans of basketball, systematically kept begging our mother to find us some tickets for the games. She attempted sporadically to call around for extra tickets, but all to no avail. Her efforts drastically increased when Yugoslavia advanced to the quarterfinal game, and my brother and I kept applying the pressure.

She reached out to Goran, a close family friend who enjoyed deep ties with the executive board of Yugoslav Basketball Association. He apologetically informed her that the game was of utmost interest and significance, and there was little he could do except convey the issue to Tony, one of the highest ranking officials in the Yugoslav Basketball Association.

When he repeated Tony's real name and surname, my mother smiled and replied, "Please just tell him it's for my two boys. I know him personally; we went to school together in Montenegro".

When Goran located Tony that day, he ignored my mother's instructions and instead tried using my father's name as leverage. He pleaded, "Hey Tony, I need you to find me two tickets for tonight's game! It's very urgent! It's for Arkan's twin boys and I am in a bad predicament. I can't tell their mother I was unable to accommodate such a request."

After hearing who the tickets were for, Tony cut him off swiftly and responded, "Look, I Don't care if they are Arkan's sons! I will find the tickets only because they are Natalija's children."

As strange as it sounds, having a mother with a humble and kindhearted reputation can clearly exceed having a father with a formidable and fearsome one.

Nevertheless, two tickets were delivered to our house an hour later.

43. " Rade is our friend"

"Keep your friends close, but your enemies closer" – Michael Corleone (excerpt from the movie *The Godfather*).

My father bragged constantly that he was a rich man when it came to an array of quality friends. However, the truth of the matter is, a majority of my father's true friends had deserted him throughout the nineties. It is no secret that a great number of his close friends have been killed. At the end of his life, he was surrounded by a group of people who pretended there was genuine friendship involved, but they only stuck around for their own profitable interests.

My father had a large stake in a lucrative oil business. The business was legitimate, as he possessed all forms of licenses and paid regular tax on all of his profits. (He primarily used this influx of money to effectively pay stipends to the families of deceased and incarcerated former soldiers who served in the Serbian Volunteer Guard). If his soccer club was his primary form of bread and butter, this oil business was something of a steady monthly income to cover his high overhead.

My father was in his office at the Obilic Stadium when he received some disturbing news. A controversial businessman (whose life was spared in the mid – 90s by my father's direct involvement) succeeded in preventing my father's oil cisterns from crossing the border into Serbia. This businessman managed to pull this through his contacts in the highest echelon of state officials. (It is believed this was done in retaliation over his tobacco smuggling business that was supposedly being confiscated earlier in the year.)

Upon hearing the news, my father became furious. He immediately rushed to the border with his assistant to see why his oil trucks were not allowed to cross into Serbia. Just as he was pondering his next move, his arch nemesis and the chief of State Security, Rade Markovic, phoned in to offer his assistance. My father gladly accepted and after the "confusion" was sorted out, the crossing point was opened again and the oil cistern poured back in.

On the way back to Belgrade, my father exulted in joy, "See, **Rade is our friend**! You know how much we hated him, but we were badly mistaken."

"With all due respect, my Komandant," his assistant interjected, "when was such an enemy a friend?"

Upon hearing this, my father went totally berserk. He furiously cussed at him, claiming Rade Markovic was finally their friend. He failed to grasp the devious and well thought-out plan formulated by the chief, whose main intention was to make my father lower his guard.

The devious plan seemed to work immediately. Thinking that his biggest arch-nemesis had become his friend, my father lowered his guard and his alertness from danger that had kept him alive for over 47 years.

It was a chill Saturday on this 15th of January when my father got inside his bulletproof Chevy suburban. Totally oblivious to the fact that a few unsuccessful murder attempts on his life had taken place in the past few months, h found himself in jovial mood as he was on his way to InterContinental Hotel. He was about to sell his star player to an Italian football giant for 15 million dollars. He felt confident the hotel was his safe destination, especially because a Chinese delegation was presiding there that particular day, so he knew it was full of police and state security agents.

Rade is our friend.

It is with this state of mind that he stepped inside the hotel. He never realized that just as he lowered his guard and alertness, he entered a real den. The wild dogs already awaited him as security cameras were disabled and a mop up team was already in place nearby.

Shots were fired shortly thereafter and the rest is all history.

44. "We have always protected our women"

One afternoon in 1997 I was returning home with my father from Hotel Jugoslavija, where he owned a casino and a fitness spa. Long before his primary office of operations was built adjacently to the Obilic Stadium, my father had used a spare table in the back of the casino to conduct all his daily business.

As we neared the bridge across the Sava, I took time to explain to my father a mishap that had just occurred between my former girlfriend and me.

"Hey Dad, I got some problems with women. Can you help me out?" "Of course, son," he ecstatically responded," I'll be more than happy to advise you in this scope."

I remarked how my former girlfriend had totally embarrassed me in front of some girls when she walked up to them and disclosed that I was only 13, and not 15 as I had told them earlier. I described how angry I became, and was so close to spilling my milkshake on her. He cut me right off to reveal, "You know the Raznatovic clan has always protected their women and are famous for it. One time when I was in Malmo with my first wife, three large intoxicated sailors began blurting out inappropriate comments to her. I jumped in the middle, pulled her to the side, and advised them to back off. When they surrounded me, I took out my mini Smith & Wesson pistol, the same one that James Bond carried. They started laughing outrageously thinking it was a toy. I tried firing a warning shot in the air, but I realized I was out of bullets. I had no choice but to throw the gun and started brawling with the three of them. When the police and ambulance arrived after ten minutes, they were quick to witness four men lying on the floor while covered in a huge pile of blood."

"Oh Wow, Dad," I remarked, "So if you fought the three of them, then obviously one of those guys on the floor was you! What a good story."

"You should always be the most protective of your sisters", he continued. "When I was in fifth grade, a well-known bully who was in eighth grade began mistreating your aunt Mima. I jumped in and got in a fight with him, and got my ass kicked so badly that I ended up staying in the hospital overnight."

"Well, At least you tried," I reasoned, "I am sure others noted your effort and bravery." "They sure did!" he replied enthusiastically, "but this was not the end of it. The following week when I recovered, I waited for him outside of his building all day with the biggest cinderblock I could find. When I saw him, I ran and hit him with the brick so hard that he landed on the floor, semiconscious! I stood directly on top of him, looked at his frightened, weary eyes and told him never to go near my sister, again!"

"Good," I replied. "I told you, Son, we have always protected our women."

45. "Founding of the Guard"

In November of 1990, my father was arrested with three others by the Croatian Authorities right by Dvor-Na-Uni. His vehicle contained Heckler & Koch automatic rifles, pistols, and grenades. He was immediately transferred to Zagreb, and accused of intent to incite an armed rebellion against the governing authorities. He was sentenced to two years in the notorious Remetinec Prison.

I recall how every time we wondered about our father's whereabouts we were told that "he was abroad, selling toys." We would correspond with him on a weekly basis, and we caught our mother traveling incognito to Zagreb every week with my 4 month old sister to visit him. She was visibly distressed and troubled during the whole time our father was "abroad." (He once sent us a postcard from Zagreb with the InterContinental Hotel depicted on the front. He even circled a random window on the picture and convinced us that's where he stayed.)

No matter how well hidden and concealed the predicament with our father was from our young ears, we could sense the tension intensifying in the house.

Things had drastically changed one day when my brother and I were forbidden to leave the house. Two men began escorting us to school on a daily basis. One carried a red duffle bag with a semi-automatic rifle inside and another a long silver revolver wrapped in a black plastic bag. They waited all day for us outside of our classroom to safely escort us back home. (We were told ten years later that the new Croatian Authorities had published names of all hardline Croatian Ustasha Émigrés who my dad had supposedly assassinated when he was employed by Tito's notorious Secret Service. Following these events, vengeful threats began arriving at his jail cell, some threatening to kidnap and kill his twin boys.)

One afternoon, our mother rushed to our room and hurried us to shower and dress nicely. We hadn't seen her so excited and cheerful the entire year. An influx of family and friends began crowding inside our house. We couldn't believe it.

Dad is coming home!

Everyone cheered when the news arrived that his chartered plane had just touched down at Belgrade Airport. There were more than two hundred people in our house feasting on lamb, cheese, and various cold cuts while sipping on homemade slivovitz and brandy.

When my father's convoy arrived outside of our house, he received a hero's welcome. As soon as he exited the vehicle, he famously declared, "Let me make this clear to all! Now that I am free, I will gather my own army of volunteers and we will defend this sacred land and our people to the last man."

October 11th, 1991, happened to be the official day his Serbian Volunteer Guard was founded. They fought some of the harshest and most epic battles of the Yugoslav wars.

The guard was officially disbanded in 1996. However, the great majority of the elite Super Tigrovi personnel were assimilated into a newly created unit controlled by the State.

Their official name was Jedinica za specijalne Operacije. They came to be better known as the Red Berets.

46. "Discipline is key to everything"

One of the requests I receive most often is to describe an instance when my father disciplined me so "effectively" that it taught me a lifelong lesson.

I recall this particular event very well and not due to the brutal beating I received, but because I wasn't the only perpetrator involved.

Spring in Belgrade brought the most pleasant weather throughout the year. Our old residence in Ljutice Bogdana Street was a modest two-story, 4 bedroom house with a splendid backyard. Every spring, before summer would unleash its unbearable heat, our backyard would host small scale get-togethers with some of our closest friends and family.

The Kalezic family had been coming to our home since I was a toddler. The father Zoran, was a famous singer who my dad had known for quite some time. His wife, Verica, was one of the most humble and loving persons we had ever known, and my mom cherished her friendship to a great extent. Their son, Filip, was a mischievous kid three years my senior. My twin brother Nikola was more reserved and standoffish when it came to hanging out with Filip, but I have always enjoyed his company and often felt as if he was my older brother.

That joyful afternoon, we were feasting on my mom's famous proja (Serbian cornbread) and sarma (stuffed cabbage rolls) that she had prepared for everyone. As the dinner was coming to a close, Filip turned to me and my brother and whispered, "Hey guys, this is getting boring. Let's go do something."

"Like what?" my brother cautiously wondered. "Let's go play hide and seek. You, Nikola, stay downstairs and count, and Vojin and I will go hide."

So as Nikola started counting to 30, Filip rushed upstairs and I followed close behind. He entered my parents' bedroom with no hesitation.

"Filip, we are not allowed to go in this room," I pleaded, "my Dad is gonna kill us." "Don't worry. We are just here for a bit until Nikola finds us," Filip replied.

He opened their closet, and he stood staring in disbelief. I rushed to see at what he was staring.

WOW! Look at that!

Now I know why this room was off limits to us!

The closet was full of deadly weapons! I picked up a rifle that seemed to have a silencer with a guided red laser dot. Filip picked up a modern bow rifle, yes with actual bows in it. We were astonished. I asked Filip if he knew why my father had this secret stash, upon which he replied, "I think my dad mentioned that there might be a war coming against Tudjman's Ustashas and that in case they reach Belgrade, we will kill them all."

At that moment, my brother burst in and saw us playing with these weapons. He quickly ran off to report his observation to my dad.

We are dead!

Not even a minute later, my dad dashed in just as we were closing the closet door. With no hesitation, he immediately started slapping us in the face and violently kicking us in our butts, switching between Filip and myself. He screamed cuss words at us as he was teaching us a lesson, and I still recollect Filip's teary face staring at me. I was wailing excessively.

"You monkeys have no idea how dangerously you put your lives at risk just now!" he affirmed. "These are real weapons, not toys! You should know as kids NEVER to touch these weapons."

We tried to apologize, but my father would hear none of it and continued, "It's our fault as parents spoiling you kids, and you think you can do whatever you want. Well now you learned a lesson and you'll think twice before touching real weapons."

As he walked towards the backyard, he added, "This is a military household and discipline is key to everything!"

My father instilled this rigorous discipline in all around those him – whether they were in his army, casino, soccer club, or household.

47. "I AM THE BOARD"

It is quite fair to declare that Football Club Obilic utterly consumed the last four years of my father's life. After witnessing the lucrative multi-billion dollar business of such nature on a global scale, one would surely not question the time, money and effort a club owner must undertake in order to reap the fruits of a colossal investment of that particular caliber.

After acquiring the club in 1996, my father instantly embarked on expanding the resources and strengthening the pillars in order to realize his immediate short term goal - threaten the two dominant horses in the race by becoming the champion. He proudly bragged how Obilic was "the true Serbian Club," founded in 1924, while the "neighbors" were founded under communist authorities in 1945. He relished in proving that a tiny, disciplined, and well organized club could achieve glory on the grandest scale.

On paper, Obilic functioned as a legitimate, western-style football organization consisting of a president, executive board, technical and managerial staff, as well as players who played for the club. Of course, my father was the alpha and omega of this enterprise, and he personally controlled and micromanaged every possible position or role in the club (even the coaching one).

Defeat was an experience he loathed. On rare occasions when Obilic would lose a game, the coach would invariably be held accountable. When Obilic lost two games in a row, the coach was sacked.

I will never forget when a coach verbally protested my father's decision to remove him as head of the club. He was in such a profound shock that he openly confronted my father, "You cannot fire me! The executive board has to make a decision whether to continue my work at this club or not."

After staring at him in complete disbelief, my father snapped back, "I AM THE BOARD!" He loudly declared, "There is no other board here! Trust me when I tell you - You are fired!"

Later on in the evening, I took this occasion to compare his answer to the famed Bourbon King Louis XIV who famously declared, "L'État, c'est moi" ("I am the state").

My father smiled back at me and replied, "That is correct, son! He was in sole charge of France, and I am in sole charge of Obilic."

48."That was the best day of my life"

The last birthday my brother and I spent in my father's presence was on August, 31, 1999. My brother and I were turning sixteen, and every year we would organize a massive bash for all of our friends and family. We were afraid how our father was going to react when we request some hard liquor and beer for the event because he was an epic adversary of liquor, drugs, and nicotine. We decided the wisest move would be to just note it on the list that contained all other arrangements for the party.

He took a moment to sit down with us to discuss the necessary birthday preparations. When we presented the list, we crossed our fingers he was going to approve it without any reservations. As soon as he spotted the alcohol on the list, he glared at us and sternly warned, "Don't piss me off, you two asses! You want beer and alcohol for your party? You are only turning 16!"

"That's all for our friends who drink," I argued, "you know Nikola and I only drink juices and Coca-Cola!" "I don't give a damn about others!" He then said, "There will be no liquor or beer at the party, understood?"

Great! Might as well just serve cookies and milk!

It took him a minute to calm down as he was skimming through the rest of the list. I suppose he felt a bit of contrition realizing how upset his twins were. He explained, "You guys wanna know something? The only time I ever drank alcohol was when you two were born!
He began shaking his head, quickly realizing how much we had grown.

Time flies.

His phone kept ringing, but he refused to even see who was calling him. "Sixteen years ago," he recalled, "I was so overjoyed with delight and euphoria that when I toasted to your health, I chugged the whole glass of red wine!"

He put his arms around us and then continued, "Nobody knows what it's like when God Almighty grants you two male heads in one shot."

He grinned, nodded his head, and acknowledged, "That was the best day of my life."

49. "I should have never swayed into Politics"

People still argue what precisely triggered my father's decision to enter the world of politics. Some claim it was the pressure from the ruling Serbian Socialist Party in order to sway a substantial amount of votes from the right wing radicals. Others argue the Serbian people of Kosovo portrayed him as the next Milos Obilic (a 14th century Serbian hero) and therefore demanded him to represent them. The other reason might have been the power of his own ego and an insurmountable thirst for glory and fame that yielded this unpractical decision to run for parliament.

When he founded the party, he gathered a considerable deal of Serbian intellectuals and academics. Even though he was a poor orator and public speaker, his immense rallies, advertisements, and celebrity endorsements provided him with the much needed publicity. He seemed confident, and his spirits remained high until the very last day of the campaign.

However, one person who had never endorsed him was my mother, Natalija. Known for sheltering herself and all of her children from the media exposure, she took time to advise him often, "Zeljko, you have no experience in politics. It's a difficult and dangerous game. People see you as a warrior and patriot, not as a politician."

My father, hardheaded and confident as he was, brushed her aside and believed his party would capture at least ten percent of the total votes. I recall how serious his demeanor would be at times; he actually brainstormed his speeches early in the morning while eating raw eggs (believing it would make his speech more flawless).

He tested his true oratory and debate skills when he agreed to appear on a TV show with the leader of the hardline radicals, Vojislav Seselj. Their relationship plummeted from comrades-in-arms to inclement political rivals. Seselj began bombarding my father about his past, even mentioned, "You have worn more socks on your head than your feet." My father had no ample reply except to expose his charismatic smile and hope for the live show to come to a speedy conclusion.

Despite the heavy campaigning and spending a fortune of his own wealth, the election results cemented a humbling defeat for his party. His official list of candidates even failed to reach the minimum quota to enter the parliament.

So furious was my father, he blamed the ruling party for supposedly stealing half a million of his votes. So hardheaded was he at times that he could never admit fault and constantly searched for a scapegoat in others. Blame had to be put on somebody for the crushing defeat.

He never admitted mistakes. He was always right.

Nonetheless, the following night was the first and perhaps only time I have heard my father openly admit fault and accept blame. He arrived home that evening remorsefully confessed to my mother, "Natalija, you were right all along. I should have never strayed into politics."

Five years later, I asked him once if he would ever like to be president of the country. He instantly replied, "Politics is the one battle in life I never managed to win."

50. "Blood is NOT Water"

One of the things I enjoyed doing the most was sitting with my father once a week in our living room and watch films. We were both fascinated with war movies, and when a film about Napoleon Bonaparte was playing our eyes seemed glued to the television.

We were acutely impressed with this short yet brave Empereur, who brought exceptional glory and fame to every Frenchman for centuries to come. I suggested how courage was the fundamental trait of every famed hero in history. This statement further enlivened my father, who quickly constituted, "Talking about bravery - did you know, Son, that our Raznatovic family has bred the finest and boldest heroes for centuries?"

"No, didn't know that," I admitted.

"How did you not know that?" he jumped. "My great-grandfather Jokelja returned home from battle once with seventeen Turkish heads he personally severed! He even received a medal of honor from the ruler of Montenegro for his bravery and service to the homeland!"

"Oh wow," I exclaimed, "I had no idea."

"My grandfather Mihailo," he bragged, "honorably defended the retreat of the Serbian army at Mojkovac during the First World War! And you know my father, Veljko, liberated Kosovo with his partisans and met your grandmother Slavka in one of the fascist concentration camps!"

"Yes, I knew that."

"And you know my uncle Vojin, who you were named after, is one of the greatest heroes of our family?"

"No Dad, tell me the story!" I anxiously demanded.

"Well, he was the local resistance leader in Montenegro, and the fascists finally captured him after he was betrayed by one of his people. They convened the whole town to the main square, where he was summarily executed in front of his mother and the entire family. But as they led him through the wheat fields to the execution site, he made sure he didn't step on any of the crops. When the fascist soldiers mocked and wondered why he was so careful about wheat, he proudly declared that "this wheat is going to feed a new hero who will avenge my death and liberate this land from all of you fascist scum!"

I stood silent, attempting to process the heroic deed of the person whose name I carried. My father proudly looked at me and resolutely declared, "Blood is NOT water!"

Glossary of People

Josip Broz "Tito" - A Yugoslav Communist resistance leader during WWII. Ruled Yugoslavia with an Iron Fist from 1945 - 1980.

Slobodan Milosevic - President of Serbia and the newly formed Yugoslavia (Serbia and Montenegro). One of the main protagonists in the breakup of Yugoslavia and the subsequent wars that followed. Ousted by a popular revolution in 2000. Died in the Hague Tribunal in 2006.

Radomir "Rade" Markovic - Head of the feared State Security Service (DB) from 1998 - 2001. One of the chief organizers and planners of my father's murder. Currently serving a prison sentence in Serbia.

Svetlana Raznatovic "Ceca" - The most popular folk singer in the Balkans. Married my father in 1995. They have two children together, Veljko and Anastasija.

Borislav Pelevic - One of the high ranking officials in my father's Volunteer Guard and the Serbian Unity Party. Capitalized on my father assassination to advance personal goals and agenda.

Zoran Djindjic - Former opposition leader, mayor of Belgrade and the Prime Minister of Serbia from 2001 until his assassination in 2003.

Radovan Stojicic "Badza" - former high ranking General of the Serbian Police and the deputy minister of the Interior. Gunned down in 1997.

Radovan Karadzic - Former Leader of the Bosnian Serbs during the Bosnian War. Currently facing charges in the International Court of Justice in the Hague.

Ratko Mladic - Former Chief of Staff of the Bosnian Serb Military Forces during the conflict. Currently facing charges in the International Court of Justice in the Hague.

Franjo Tudjman - Former President of Croatia. Another main protagonist during the breakup of Yugoslavia. Died in 1999.

Vuk Draskovic - Leader of the Serbian Opposition movement in the early 1990's. Milosevic's main rival on the domestic political scene. Still involved in the Serbian Politics.

Vojislav Seselj - The leader of the ultra-right nationalist Serbian Radical Party. Currently facing charges in the Hague Tribunal.

About the Author

Vojin Raznatovic was born in Belgrade, Serbia in 1983. His family moved to Athens, Greece when he was ten years old. He graduated from High School in 2001, where he was a class president. He completed his B.A. in History from Loyola Marymount University in Los Angeles, where he was a Dean's List student. He holds a great passion for acting, singing, boxing and surfing. This was his debut book. His next novel, *The Serbian Dream*, is due in late 2015. He lives in California.

www.facebook.com/jogiraznatovic
www.twitter.com/VOJINRAZNATOVIC
vojinraznatovic@gmail.com

Coming Soon

December 2015

Printed in Great Britain
by Amazon